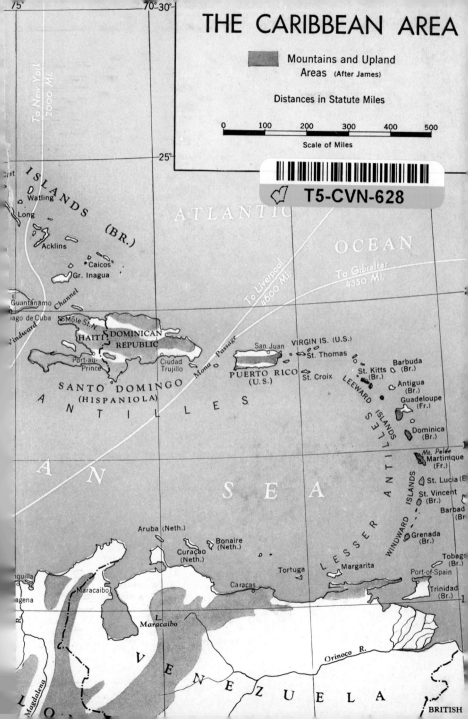

THE CARIBBEAN AREA

Mountains and Upland
Areas (After James)

Distances in Statute Miles

0   100   200   300   400   500
Scale of Miles

T5-CVN-628

ATLANTIC

OCEAN

To New York
2000 Mi.

75°   70°30'

25°

ISLANDS (BR.)

Watling

Long

Acklins

Caicos

Gr. Inagua

To Liverpool
4600 Mi.

To Gibraltar
4350 Mi.

Guantánamo

Channel

iago de Cuba

Mole St. N.

Windward

HAITI   DOMINICAN
REPUBLIC

Port-au-
Prince

Ciudad
Trujillo

SANTO DOMINGO
(HISPANIOLA)

A   N   T   I   L   L   E   S

A
N

Mona Passage

San Juan

PUERTO RICO
(U.S.)

St. Croix

VIRGIN IS. (U.S.)

St. Thomas

St. Kitts
(Br.)

Barbuda
(Br.)

Antigua
(Br.)

Guadeloupe
(Fr.)

Dominica
(Br.)

LEEWARD ISLANDS

L   E   S   S   E   R   A   N   T   I   L   L   E   S

Mt. Pelee
Martinique
(Fr.)

St. Lucia (Br

St. Vincent
(Br.)

Barbad
(Br

WINDWARD ISLANDS

S   E   A

Aruba (Neth.)

Curaçao
(Neth.)

Bonaire
(Neth.)

Tortuga

Caracas

Margarita

Grenada
(Br.)

Tobag
(Br.)

Port-of-Spain

Trinidad
(Br.)

nquilla

agena

Maracaibo

L.
Maracaibo

Magdalena

V   E   N   E   Z   U   E   L   A

Orinoco R.

BRITISH

THE AMERICAN FOREIGN POLICY LIBRARY

SUMNER WELLES, EDITOR
DONALD C. MCKAY, ASSOCIATE EDITOR

The United States and the Caribbean

LONDON : GEOFFREY CUMBERLEGE

OXFORD UNIVERSITY PRESS

THE
UNITED STATES
AND
The Caribbean

By

Dexter Perkins, *1889-*

HARVARD UNIVERSITY PRESS
Cambridge, Massachusetts
1947

MAPS PREPARED UNDER THE CARTOGRAPHIC
DIRECTION OF ARTHUR H. ROBINSON

PRINTED AND BOUND BY NORWOOD PRESS
J. S. CUSHING CO.; BERWICK AND SMITH CO.
NORWOOD, MASSACHUSETTS, U.S.A.

CONTENTS

MAP

INTRODUCTION

The independent nations of the Caribbean area are among those of the American Republics with which the people of the United States are least familiar. It is true that tourists swarm to Havana every winter, that the cities of Colón and of Panama are well known to the voyagers who pass through the Panama Canal, and that air travel has enabled many Americans to obtain a superficial acquaintance with the capitals of Central America, the Dominican Republic, and Haiti. With the gradual extension of the Pan American Highway, as it links Mexico, the Central American Republics, and Panama, a better means of knowing their neighbors of the Caribbean will be presented to many thousands of Americans.

But to most of us the national problems, the political life, the manner of being, the culture and the economy of these nine smaller republics of the Western Hemisphere are still a closed book. It is for that reason that Dexter Perkins' penetrating and comprehensive analysis of the Caribbean Republics of the Americas has been written at a peculiarly opportune moment.

The importance to the people of this country of hemispheric solidarity is at last beginning to be appreciated at its true value.

In the development of any strong regional system of the Americas, the Republics of the Caribbean must always play an outstanding part. From the standpoint of hemispheric defense they occupy a strategic position which is of vital significance. Without their collaboration any adequate protection of the Panama Canal would be impossible, and the air and naval bases established by the United States during the Second World War as a result of the destroyers-bases agreement reached with Great Britain would be of scant value. The loyal and unwavering support rendered by all of these republics to the United States after the Japanese attack upon Pearl Harbor was of prime importance in enabling the United States to defend itself as well as in making it possible for its armed forces to move effectively in helping to defend the other Americas.

From the economic viewpoint the potential resources of all these nations, as Professor Perkins makes it abundantly clear, are almost unlimited. We think of them all too often as countries which can raise only such tropical products as sugar, bananas, and coffee. Yet because of their mineral wealth, because of the fertility of their soil, and because of the great diversity in their regional climatic conditions, increased capital investment and up-to-date economic planning would enable them to supply United States markets with a vast number of essential commodities that we now import from remote regions of the earth. Any such enlargement and diversification of the trade between the United States and these neighbor republics would prove to be of immediate benefit to the economy of this country by rapidly raising living standards throughout the Caribbean area, and thereby correspondingly increasing the capacity of all the citizens of these countries to buy goods exported from the United States.

By no means the least valuable aspect of Professor Perkins' book is the opportunity it affords to the average reader here to familiarize himself with political conditions in these other American states. It is within this area, of course, that former administrations in Washington so often resorted to constant interference and even to armed intervention. No aspect of our earlier inter-American policy has done more harm than this to the welfare of the entire hemisphere. The intervention policy not only aroused the suspicion that the United States was bent upon a course of continental imperialism, but has provoked resentments and antagonisms that are still latent now, many years after the adoption of the Good-Neighbor Policy. It has done equal harm by retarding the political self-reliance of many of the peoples of these republics. It has all too often checked the growth of a national democracy, forged to meet the individual needs of each people. Yet even so, no more advanced democracy is to be found in the Americas today than that created in the Republic of Costa Rica. And the liberal political institutions which are gradually becoming established in a majority of these states are helping to expedite the consolidation of democracy throughout the Western Hemisphere.

Democracy will never be firmly established in any part of the Americas as a result of alien interference or coercion. It will continue to grow stronger as industrialization increases, as living standards are correspondingly raised, as freedom of information and of expression become more secure, and the solidarity of all of the American Republics becomes more firmly crystallized.

I have spent many years in the Republics described in this book. There is nowhere to be found a greater popular devotion to the cause of individual liberty. There is nowhere to be found greater kindliness nor a more genuine spirit of hospitality. And surely there are few parts of the world which can rival these countries in their natural beauty or in the charm and graciousness of their national culture.

Professor Perkins has written with exceptional knowledge and experience. He is intimately familiar with the countries which he describes. I hope that this book will persuade many citizens of the United States to visit, and thus to know for themselves, these close neighbors presented in it.

Sumner Welles

PREFACE

With regard to international relations, there are two schools of thought to be avoided. On the one hand are the romantics, who seem to believe that good will is a universal solvent of international difficulties, who cannot or will not appreciate the role that physical power plays and has always played in diplomacy, and who are blind to the influences conferred upon a people by vast resources and extensive territory. On the other hand are the cynics, who believe, or seem to believe, that international politics is nothing but the struggle of selfish forces, and that the only rule in international affairs is for those who have to keep their power, and those to take who can. Both these views are refuted by the actual course of human events. It is, of course, true, in the world in which we live, that force is the ultimate arbiter, and that no nation is willing to renounce it to the extent of leaving itself unprotected against others. But it is not true that nations act without regard to other considerations than those of pure power. In particular, democratic nations, and perhaps most of all the English-speaking democracies, are powerfully affected by what they conceive to be moral considerations and by a desire to produce a world society better than that of the past. Nowhere has this been better demonstrated than in the policy of the United States towards the numerous small states that are its neighbors. To set forth this story, as I have sought to do in this little volume, is to make clear the manner in which a great nation may make moderate use of its physical power and take a long, rather than a short, view of its national interests. Flaws in the record of course there are; but if it be the case that the self-restraint of the most powerful states is one of the best assurances for the future, then the record of the United States in the Caribbean is one of which to be proud. It has been a pleasure here to analyze it.

In the preparation of this book, I must first of all thank the editors of this series, Mr. Sumner Welles, whose practical experience and knowledge of the Caribbean are profound, and Professor Donald C. McKay for their helpful and penetrating criticism. In the gathering of materials, very great assistance was rendered by my former student, Mr. Richard C. Wade, who brought great enthusiasm and industry to the work, and by Douglas Parks of the staff of the Pan American Union. Finally, as in the preparation of other works, I owe much to the painstaking and unstinted efforts of my secretary, Miss Marjorie Gilles.

The University of Rochester   Dexter Perkins
August 7, 1947

The United States and the Caribbean

1. The Countries and Their Peoples

The area of the Caribbean is not difficult to define. It is fixed in the most definite way by the islands and by the Continental mass that encircle, and make of this body of water, in the broadest sense of the word, an inland sea. On the north, for example, if we wish to trace its periphery, we may begin with Cuba, by far the largest island of the region, stretching some seven hundred and thirty miles from east to west, and at its western end not far removed from the mainland of Florida. A narrow passage separates this important state from the island of Santo Domingo, far smaller and, from the historian's point of view, far less significant. Here have grown up, however, two of the most picturesque independent republics of the New World, on the western side of the black state of Haiti, and on the east, occupying about two-thirds of the surface of the island, the Dominican Republic. Taken together, these two communities extend the northern boundary of the Caribbean nearly four hundred miles farther to the eastward. Separated by a narrow passage from the next important land mass still farther east, the so-called Mona Passage, Haiti and the Dominican Republic are neighbors to the American territory of Puerto Rico, about one hundred miles long at its widest point, and still farther on are the American-owned Virgin Islands, which are, of course, still smaller. Thence in a broad arc, over 500 miles in extent, there stretches the chain of the Antilles, mostly British, but with Guadeloupe and Martinique in the hands of France, and beyond all of these the British possession of Trinidad, off the coast of Venezuela. From this point we may follow the coast of South America westward, first Venezuela, then Colombia, then Panama, and from the Canal northward along the eastern shore of Central America, with Costa Rica, Nicaragua, Honduras, and Guatemala, all bounding the inland sea, and with the gap finally almost closed by the Mexican peninsula of Yucatan. From the tip of Yucatan it is again only a fairly narrow passage that brings us back to Cuba.

It is possible, then, to speak of the Caribbean region as a distinct geographical unit. But for the purposes of this particular study the term must be somewhat more limited. It is obvious, for example, that where matters of foreign policy are concerned, the independent states of the region are of more significance than the colonial dependencies. The British islands of the Caribbean have recently become of special importance to the United States through the creation of the Anglo-American Caribbean Commission, and through the acquisition, by the famous destroyer-bases deal of September 1940, of American bases all the way from Bermuda to Trinidad; but even taking this fact into account they must necessarily concern us far less than the self-governing republics whose names have already been enumerated. But some of these also lie beyond the range of this study. Colombia and Venezuela form a part of northern South America, and may be more conveniently examined in the volume of this series which deals with that region. Mexico is of such transcendent importance in American diplomacy that it deserves, and has received, a volume to itself. This leaves us, then, nine independent communities around which our analysis must center, the island states of Cuba, Haiti, and Santo Domingo, the republic of Panama, and the communities of Central America, including, perforce, one country which does not front on the Caribbean at all, the little republic of El Salvador. In dealing with this region it is possible to generalize, and also to differentiate, along certain broad lines. And in all of it the United States has special interests which we shall wish to analyze in detail.

Let us first look, however, at the fundamentals of the geography of the region. It is needless to say, at the outset, that it represents one of the great highways of oceanic communication in the world. To pass from the Atlantic to the Pacific through the Panama Canal one must pass through the Caribbean. The trade of this region is increasing, and will increase. When the Canal was opened in August of 1914 there passed through its locks and through the waters of Lake Gatun for the rest of that year and 1915 no less than 4,888,000 tons of shipping; by 1920 the figure was 9,372,000 tons; by 1940 it was 27,299,000 tons. What the Mediterranean is to the Old World, the Caribbean is to the New. What Suez has been to England in the past, Panama is to the United States. Strategically, and commercially, there are few more important areas than the one we are about to study. Time and technology, as we shall see, have altered and may continue to alter some of the elements of the defense problem; but no changes that we at present foresee will substantially diminish its importance.

The second fundamental generalization that is to be made with regard to the geography of the regions of the Caribbean is that the whole area is within the tropics, and is beset by the problems that have particularly to do with tropical conditions. But it is very easy to misunderstand what these problems are. There are many persons who assume, for example, that when we speak of the tropics we speak of a region of intolerable heat, of a drenching rainy season deleterious to health, of pathless jungle, and of human beings constantly enervated by the conditions which confront them, and incapable of any such advance as occurs in the temperate zones. Such a picture would have elements of truth, but it would by no means represent the whole truth. There are, of course, parts of the region which are decidedly difficult from the viewpoint of the white man. The east coast of Central America, for example, is likely to be pretty torrid for a good part of the year. But the climate of Cuba, to take one example, is really one of the most delightful in the world. And one of the things that is not to be forgotten about tropical lands is that the temperature naturally varies with the elevation, and that a country whose coastal plain may not be very attractive from the climatic point of view may be fine in its upland areas. This, indeed, is precisely the case with regard to a large part of the Caribbean zone. Cuba, it is true, is, except at its eastern end, fairly level, and its comfort derives from the winds that blow across its relatively narrow width, rather than from its mountains. But the two republics of Haiti and the Dominican Republic are by no means flat, and some relief from the heat can be found in their mountainous areas. Still more is this the case with Central America. The republics of this region, indeed, are traversed by what is virtually an extension of the Andean chain. It is precisely in the highlands thus formed that a large part of the life of these little states is centered. And here the temperatures are very agreeable. San José, the capital of Costa Rica, for example, has a mean temperature that stays at about seventy degrees all the year round. Tegucigalpa, the capital of Honduras, is described by an eminent American geographer as having one of the most pleasing climates in the world. Guatemala City, the capital of the state of the same name, is also peculiarly favored, and the mountainous part of the country is certainly not oppressively hot; indeed, it can be uncomfortably cold. It is, therefore, wholly wrong to think of these regions as if they were without exception regions of oppressive temperature, enervating to those who dwell in them.

It is necessary, also, to say a word or two about the alternation of the seasons in the tropics. That there is a dry season, and a wet season, is a fact generally known. But it is not so commonly realized that the wet season, in many parts of the area, is one in which it rains only a few hours a day. One cannot generalize in this regard, for a very wide variety of conditions exist in the nine republics that are included in this study. But very often, as, for example, in the mountainous regions of Central America, there is a tremendous downpour during a short part of the day, and then the sun comes out again. In other words, the rainy season is a very different thing from what the words suggest. And the number of hours of sunshine in such a period may far exceed the number of hours of sunshine in some parts of the United States at any time of year.

There is another question touching the geography of tropical lands which deserves a word of comment. Is it the case, as is so often alleged, that tropical heat naturally predisposes to indolence, and that tropical countries cannot be expected to undergo the same vigorous development that takes place in temperate ones? This is a common view, and it is in a measure endorsed by very distinguished authority. The eminent geographer, Ellsworth Huntington, for example, maintains that where the means of subsistence are easily found (and this is likely, of course, to be the case in the tropics), the energy of the producing groups is likely to be diminished. But it is easily arguable that other factors explain the relatively slow tempo of development in the hotter parts of the globe. There are some very warm regions where a vigorous development is taking place, just as there are some cold ones where progress is slow. Preston James, another distinguished student of Latin America, suggests that the real difficulty lies not in the climate itself but in the diseases to which a hot climate gives rise, and which can be combated by proper public health measures. Malaria, hookworm, and other such diseases are likely to be endemic in warm countries. But no one of these diseases is without its cure, and, given a vigorous effort to deal with them, an immense amount could be done to raise the economic level of the states of the Caribbean. We shall, indeed, return to this matter later. Enough has here been said to cast reasonable doubt upon the thesis that the tropics are necessarily incapable of the kind of economic development that has taken place in more favored parts of the world. And, certainly, even if one assigned a measure of validity to such a thesis, it would still be difficult to maintain, in view of the progress made in many of these communities during the last fifty years, that an end to that progress had been reached, and that nothing more could be expected.

But what of the peoples that inhabit these various countries? What is to be said of them? Who and what are they? And precisely what is to be expected of them? There are several groups to be considered in answering this question. There are, first of all, the whites; secondly, there are the mestizos, or mixed bloods, a fusion of Spanish and Indian types; thirdly, there are the Indians; and, fourthly, there are the Negroes. We shall consider these various strains in the reverse order.

The Negro elements are, of course, most numerous in the islands of the Caribbean. Haiti, for example, with a population of around three million, is a Negro state. It came into being at the beginning of the nineteenth century through the revolt of the slaves, who formed the major part of its people, against the French planters who represented the governing class of the island. The war of extermination that then took place resulted in the virtual extinction of those of white blood. Of course, before these events took place, some admixture of race had taken place; and in the evolution of the Haitian state a distinction has grown up between the pure blacks and those with some trace of European ancestry. In the main, the governing classes are drawn from the latter group, and this has been especially true during the last thirty years, though the rule is not one without its exceptions. No matter what these distinctions, however, Haiti must be considered as a Negro state (using the term with no connotation of inferiority); and it is, of course, almost unique in the world from this point of view, its only rival, in complete independence, being the African republic of Liberia.

The other islands of the Caribbean, however, contain a numerous Negro population. In the colonial period most of these islands imported large numbers of slaves, and the descendants of these slaves remain there today. The island of Jamaica, for example, Great Britain's most important possession in the area, is overwhelmingly black; so, too, are such French possessions as Martinique and Guadeloupe; so, too, are such smaller colonies as Barbados, or the lesser Antilles, and also the American-owned Virgin Islands.

Indeed, there are only a few exceptions to the general rule. The Dominican Republic, which occupies the eastern end of the island of Santo Domingo, is a state with mixed populations; the island of Trinidad contains a number of racial groups; Cuba has only a minority of blacks; and Puerto Rico still fewer.

Let us look, especially, at the Dominican Republic and Cuba. The first of these states owes its origin to Spanish settlers who, though slaveholders, never kept such large numbers of Negroes as did the French at the other end of the island. It began its history with a white population, which was not very large but which survived the days of the servile war in Haiti and has continuously played a part in the affairs of the republic. But in the early 1820's the country was overrun by the Haitian leader, Boyer, and it remained under Haitian rule for more than twenty years. Inevitably, in such a period, a great deal of fusion took place, and a large Negro population now exists within the confines of the state. It is, of course, most numerous along what is now the Haitian-Dominican border, and in the south, rather than in the north; but it is not the dominating element, and Dominicans as a whole may certainly be said to have no desire to see it increased. There seems to be little racial prejudice as such, but there is a widespread determination not to permit submergence by the republic that is its neighbor.

As for Cuba, the Negro population of this republic is, of course, as elsewhere, descended from the slaves of the colonial epoch. It was once much more numerous in proportion to the total number of inhabitants than it is today. Cuba is one of the countries of the New World which in the nineteenth and early twentieth centuries received a very substantial white immigration, and the percentage of blacks has shrunk from over fifty in 1840 to something like twenty-seven today. It is difficult to speak with precision in such matters; no doubt there are not a few Cuban mulattoes who have been accepted as white; but the number of blacks does not seem to be increasing in relation to the total number of Cubans. In some respects the position of the Cuban Negro is much more favorable than it is in the United States. Negroes and mulattoes take an active part in political affairs; they have given some great names to Cuban politics; and they are sometimes accepted socially. There is no legal discrimination against them of the kind that exists in our own southern states; they are freely admitted to the schools and universities. But it cannot be said, despite this fact, that there is no Negro problem. Thirty years ago, for example, a part of the Negro population banded together under a vigorous leader, named Esteñoz, and sought to found a political party which was based upon color, and color alone. The movement led to a revolt, which was quickly suppressed, and which was followed by the passage of a law making the existence of such a party illegal. But, very obviously, the sense of solidarity among a colored group cannot be destroyed quite so easily. While in the main there has been no repetition of the events in 1912, the Cuban Negro may be expected to become increasingly self-conscious politically, and to attempt the amelioration of the lot of those of his own hue. The Negroes in the past have largely been at the bottom of the social scale; and in an age when there is much unrest on the part of the masses it is safe to assume that they will be heard from more and more. They are concentrated, to a substantial extent, in the eastern province of Oriente; from time to time there has been fantastic talk of an independent Negro state there; but there seems little reason to assume that things will ever go as far as that. The Cubans have, indeed, an excellent opportunity and an excellent chance to solve their racial problem by a general process of social amelioration; and while it would be foolish to deny the existence of a color problem, it would certainly be unnecessarily gloomy to paint it in highly colored terms.

Perhaps one thing more should be said. The Cuban Negro feels no special sense of community or comradeship with his Haitian brother, or with the native Jamaican. In this respect he is a Cuban first and a Negro second. And such he is likely to remain.

In addition to the Negro population of the islands, there is a certain amount of Negro population on the east coast of Central America, and in Panama. Here the great fruit companies have often preferred Negro labor to any other, and encouraged a substantial immigration. The percentage of Negroes has been recently estimated as thirteen in Panama, ten in Nicaragua, four in Costa Rica, and 2.2 in Honduras. The Central American Negro, of course, does not object to fusion with other groups, but in the main, in Honduras, in Nicaragua, and in Costa Rica, he has not been accepted by the dominant racial elements. Indeed, there is now a distinct tendency to discourage his immi-

gration. The present regime in Honduras has cut it off
entirely; the Nicaraguan government has imposed severe
restrictions upon it; and the Costa Rican government re-
stricts new Negro arrivals to the coastal provinces. All in all,
it cannot be said that the black man will receive a very
cordial welcome on the mainland of Central America. That
there are some difficult problems connected with his future
we shall soon see.

The Indian population of the states of the Caribbean is to
be found entirely upon the Continent. In the islands the
native Indian stock was practically exterminated by the
Spaniards. But, on the mainland, apart from motives of
humanity and self-interest, the conquerors could hardly
have wiped out the numerous population that there existed.
They did not even try to do so; and there are sections of
Central America today in which there still exists a pre-
Columbian culture, and many relics of the days before the
white man came to the New World.

By far the most important Indian group is that in Guatemala, where it forms certainly no less than 55 per cent of
the total population. The Guatemalan Indians are the descendants of the Mayas, and the representatives, therefore,
of one of the most ancient civilizations on the American
continent. Almost as early as the dawn of the Christian era,
the Mayas had already given evidence of substantial cultural
progress. They had a calendar which was more accurate
than the calendar of the Romans; they had a mathematical
system which included the abstract conception of zero, at
that time unknown to the West; they built roads and temples
on a substantial scale, and pyramids which have no rival outside Egypt; they developed an intensive agriculture; and
they possessed a settled political order. Some of the fundamental inventions, it is true, they missed, most notably the
use of the wheel, or the domestication of any draft animal.
But the total achievement was considerable, and forms today
a fascinating object of study to archaeologists.

The Maya culture extended from the Mexican province of Yucatan to what is now Northern Honduras. Its earliest seats were in the south, and the visitor to Guatemala can well afford, on his way to the capital from Puerto Barrios, to stop off and see the ruins of Quirigua, which date from about the seventh century. The majestic stelae of this site, with their elaborate carvings and their individualized figures, are an amazing example of the development of Mayan art. Further south, across the border in Honduras, at Copan, are elaborate temple structures, even more impressive, and the product of a very considerable degree of civilization. Later the Mayas enjoyed an era of great prosperity further north, in the region of Chichen; the total period of their development, with an interruption of some centuries, in the middle, extends over not less than thirteen or fourteen hundred years. Even today, in Guatemala, the Indians of Momostenango gather on a given day, known as the Guaxachip Bats, and there celebrate ancient rites which go back long before the Conquest. They are aware of this date without any written calendar, handing down the memory of time by oral tradition. They still worship, in private, and sometimes in public, the ancient gods; at the church in Chichicastenango the holiest place is not the high altar but the site on which there once stood a temple of the antique religion. And on the hillsides outside the town one finds altars erected, not to some Christian saint, but to the deities of the pre-Columbian world.

The Maya Indians of today appear to have none of the cultural dynamic which enabled their ancestors to build so remarkable a culture. They are sturdy, on the whole peaceable, capable of great endurance, and reasonably industrious. They live in villages of their own, and enjoy a very considerable measure of self-government. They are, of course, usually illiterate and very much attached to their ancient ways. And what, perhaps, is of more importance than any of this, they are still at that stage of development where the acquisitive instincts are far from keen. It is said of the Guatemalan Indian that he will walk for miles to carry the product of his handicraft to a market, and that when he arrives he will sell the product for precisely the same sum that he would charge if he were in his native village. His conception of life is simple, even primitive; and the alteration of his mores is a task that will take many years, one may be sure.

It will naturally occur to the reader to inquire whether in a state where the Indian forms so large a part of the population there is likely to occur a movement such as that which distinguishes the recent history of Mexico. In that country there has been, as is well known, a harking back to and a glorification of the ancient Indian culture, and this movement affects profoundly the texture of Mexican politics. Will the same thing take place in Guatemala? The answer to this question cannot be a completely unqualified one. The situation in the Central American republic is not similar to that in its northern neighbor. In Mexico there is a land problem, and a great one. In Guatemala, which is still sparsely settled, there is no such question. One of the main sources of discontent in the one country is therefore absent in the other. Until population increase has continued on a considerable scale, this situation is not likely to change. But, on the other hand, there is, in the last decade or two, a perceptible alteration in the attitude of the governing classes towards the Indian. For almost all of the first century of Guatemalan history, the attitude of most administrations was indifferent, or contemptuous. The Indian was expected to be exploited, and the central question was what was the most convenient way to exploit him. Even Barrios, the most liberal of Guatemalan presidents, appears to have taken a point of view such as that just described. Occasionally there would be flickerings of a reform movement; but they were no more than flickerings. In the course of the last two decades, however, there has been a distinct change. The shameless advantage taken of the Indian through a system of debt slavery aroused indignation within the country, and criticism outside. President Ubico, who came to the presidency in 1931, and was only recently ousted from power, was genuinely interested in the Indians. His frequent presidential addresses were often concerned with the redress of the Indian grievances. He made the Indians more conscious of the place of government in their lives than they have ever been before, and he sought to remedy the worst abuses of the economic system under which they often remained in debt peonage for years at a time. His attitude was not merely personal—it was typical of a change that was taking place in Guatemalan opinion. And it was, of course, bound to have some effect upon the Indians themselves. Indeed, the spirit of social amelioration which is characteristic of our time cannot fail to reach the peoples of Central America, and affect their way of life. And while the Indian is as yet on the verge of political self-consciousness, it is possible that he will inevitably become more aware of what he has a right to from government, and more insistent in demanding it. There is certainly not in Guatemala today a strong movement such as might lead to serious unrest, or bloodshed on a considerable scale; but the world moves, and the Guatemalan Indian is likely to move with it.

It is, however, necessary to say clearly what has only been hinted at in the preceding pages. The Guatemalan Indian today lives upon a very low level of economic wants and aspirations. He works largely because he is required to work by law. He is quite content, in many cases, in most, in fact, to cultivate his little garden, to enjoy his simple pleasures, and to go on in the way his fathers went on before him. There is nothing peculiar about Indian human nature that precludes the gradual development of the desire for a higher standard of living. But the process is bound to be slow, and this fact will powerfully affect the growth of the country as a whole.

In no other country of Central America, however, is there an Indian question similar to that of Guatemala. In El Salvador there is a native population of about 20 per cent, and the Indians are still largely segregated. They are industrious and efficient; indeed they are often preferred as laborers to the mixed bloods of the same social groups; but their economic status is not at all similar to that of their Maya cousins. In many cases they have little farms of their own, and they are undeniably more advanced in their economic desires than the Guatemalan Indians. There are signs of interest in them on the part of the governing classes; in December the whole country celebrates the "Day of the Indian," and children and young people dressed in authentic Indian costume walk in procession to honor their patroness, the Virgin of Guadalupe. They play a modest part in politics, but they are not a special force to be reckoned with, as matters stand today.

In the case of the other states of Central America, the Indian population is less important. It is smallest in Costa Rica, where it amounts to only 2 per cent. It is hardly larger in Nicaragua, and is, in general, concentrated in the east. The Nicaraguan Indians are perhaps most worth mentioning because of their picturesque name of the Mosquitos, and because of the part they played in Anglo-American rivalry in Central America a hundred years ago.

But in Panama the case is different. In this little country there are several Indian groups which are individual enough to deserve special mention. There are, for example, the San Blas, among the most interesting tribal groups in any part of Latin America. They live on the east coast of the republic, to the east of the canal, in an area which extends almost to the Colombian border, and are among the most colorful, the most self-sufficient, and the most orderly of any of the groups. They are short and square-shouldered, and have the high flat cheekbones, narrow slanting eyes, and straight dark hair of some Asiatic strains. They live a life similar to that of the South Sea Islanders, making long voyages in their dugout canoes, fishing with spears and bows and arrows, and maintaining plantations along the inland rivers, where they bury their dead, gather fruit, and carry on some little cultivation. They live, however, on the islands of the coast, in huts with steeply pitched palm-thatched roofs, and in villages the streets of which are of sand. They are highly independent in spirit, but periodically their chiefs visit the capital and renew their allegiance to the republic. They still are governed by their own tribal laws, however, and can be visited only under careful regulations. Even today, white men cannot remain within their residential areas after sunset. While not numerous, and lacking in any such picturesque past as characterized the Mayas, they are certainly one of the most interesting groups in any part of the Caribbean.

But there are other groups within the confines of Panama that deserve a word of mention. On the Isthmus of Darien, where Balboa first sighted the Pacific in 1513, live Indians very different from the San Blas, tall and straight, and resembling some of the tribes of South America. They paint their bodies in geometric patterns with highly colored dyes, and wear silver jewelry on a profuse scale. They occupy a region which is still very difficult to penetrate, and the adventurous visit them only through the vessels of the national tourist commission.

Finally, in Panama, there is still a third group, the Indians that inhabit the country west of the Canal and extending to the Costa Rican border. These people have had much more contact with Western civilization than the San Blas or the Indians of Darien, but they are still sufficiently distinctive, and they represent an attractive expression of the Indian spirit. Taken all together, it must be remembered, these various groups make up only a small minority of the population of the republic; but they give to Panama an element of color and variety that is certainly worth noting, and underline the fact, too often forgotten, that far nearer to us than any part of Europe there are charming bits of country that the ubiquitous American traveler has rarely troubled to see or understand.

So much for the Indian population of the Caribbean. We must next turn to the very numerous mestizo element, and attempt to appraise its importance. And as an introduction to the subject it is necessary to say that in their conquest of the Central American zone the Spaniards pursued a very different policy from the one the British were to adopt further north a hundred years later. They did not aim at the extermination of the Indian, or even at thrusting him back from a frontier line of their own; they aimed rather at incorporating him in their own polity. The reasons for this were partly mercenary and partly more disinterested; it was desired to exploit the native population; it was also desired to Christianize them. In the Caribbean islands, despite this general conception of policy, the actual results were the virtual disappearance of the native stock; but on the Continent there took place a fusion of races that is one of the salient facts in the history of the region. The mestizo, the mixture of Spaniard and Indian, is by far the most characteristic type in several of the Central American republics, and he is a type of substantial importance in all but one of them. Let us look at the figures first of all, and see what they reveal. In Guatemala mixed blood is in the neighborhood of 40 per cent. The census indeed recognizes only Ladinos, as they are called, and Indians, and it is possible that among the Ladinos may be a small number of persons of purely white blood; but of these there can hardly be many. In Honduras the mestizo group is estimated at 86 per cent, in El Salvador at 80 per cent, in Nicaragua at

68 per cent, in Costa Rica at 14 per cent, and in Panama at 58 per cent. Putting the matter another way, it forms a substantial majority of the population in all but one of these states.

What significance does this fact have in the life of the republics concerned? There are at least two generalizations that ought to be set down in answer to such a question. The first of these is that many, probably most, of these people, whatever the mixture of bloods, regard themselves as the heirs of the Spanish tradition. We shall have more to say of what that tradition implies when we come to discuss the pure white European stock in the Caribbean; but we should say here that the mass of these people speak Spanish as their mother tongue, that they share in the psychological outlook which is characteristic of Spanish peoples, and that they feel some sense of solidarity as the result of this community of origin. The second generalization is this. The term "mestizo" not only carries no connotation of an unpleasant kind in Central America, but it ought not to do so. Sometimes North Americans have curious views as to the mixture of bloods, though they of all people ought to understand how such mixtures occur. There is little reason to believe that the mixture of Spaniard and Indian has produced an inferior stock, that it is the controlling factor in the development, or in the retardation of the development, of these little states; or that it is a factor which militates against their progress in the future. There are other far more important elements as we shall see which explain the comparative backwardness of some of the Central American republics; to blame conditions on the racial mixture would be entirely and unreservedly unscientific.

In the figures that we have just noted, it will be observed that in Costa Rica the percentage of mixed stock is only 14; and that brings us to the last element in the population of the Caribbean, the white stock itself. Costa Rica is the state in which this stock is most numerous; indeed it forms a most interesting example of a preponderantly white community in the midst of populations of another type. The Indian population of this part of Central America appears never to have been very numerous; and the region was settled by Spaniards, largely from Galicia, who formed a most sturdy, industrious, and hard-working element. Their descendants are there today, and form the preponderant elements in this interesting republic. In Cuba something more than a majority of the people are of European blood, and, as has already been said, the proportion has tended to increase, at least up to the depression years that followed the crash of 1929. With the exception of these two states the white stock is nowhere more than a small minority in the area we are considering; nonexistent in Haiti; too small for separate enumeration in Guatemala and El Salvador; a mere handful, 1.8 per cent, in Honduras; more numerous, but in no case as high as 20 per cent in Nicaragua, in Panama, and in the Dominican Republic.

Despite their comparatively small numbers, however, it ought to be clearly understood that in their influence, and indeed in the fixing of the national temperament and culture, the whites of the Caribbean area are more important than hypercritical observers are apt to assume. There are, as we have seen, parts of the region in which native populations are living in a relatively primitive state which suggests only the thinnest veneer of European culture, if any such culture at all, such districts as those of rural Haiti, of Indian Guatemala, of the more remote provinces of Panama. But for the most part the white stock has fixed the cultural mold in the Caribbean; it has contributed its language; it has contributed its religion, so that everywhere the Catholic Church plays a part, though a variable one, in the national life; it has contributed its political and its social ideals. It is impossible to understand these interesting peoples if one does not bear this constantly in mind. It is impossible to treat of them sympathetically unless one ungrudgingly recognizes that they are, and that they regard themselves, as the heirs of a great civilization, and of a renowned culture. We shall see in a later chapter that there is much which justifies such a view; but it is as well in this opening chapter to issue a caveat against that supercilious sense of superiority which sometimes characterizes the intercourse and judgment of citizens of the United States towards their southern brethren.

Having analyzed the various elements that make up the population of the Caribbean, the next question that naturally suggests itself is the degree in which these populations are likely to change, in the future. Will the racial stocks be profoundly modified? Will the pattern we have traced be fundamentally altered with time? In such a state as Haiti one sees little reason to suppose that circumstances will be much different two or three decades from now from what they are today. The white strain that exists in the Haitian upper classes can hardly be expected to become stronger, for there is virtually no intermarriage with Europeans or North Americans; but the disappearance of the men of color is also a very remote possibility. In the islands of the Caribbean also the black stocks will no doubt maintain themselves, and, looking at the matter in the light of secular tendencies, there is a diminution of the small white element in such regions as Jamaica or Barbados. In the Dominican Republic, and in the states of Central America, the process of fusion of bloods that has taken place in so large a measure already is likely to be continued; the sense of racial discrimination is so weak that the preservation of a really white class is pretty difficult; yet it is remarkable that after four hundred years important elements in these little states should still regard themselves as white. In Cuba, the hostility to the immigration of blacks offers some reason to believe that the pure Negro population will slowly decrease in numbers;

it is possible also that the whites will increase by the addition of an increment from abroad. Cuba offers a more than usually attractive prospect to the immigrant; but, of course, conditions have not been such during the last two decades as to make any very substantial movement possible.

On the question of immigration, indeed, a special word should be said. Despite the keen desire for the encouragement of European immigration which has been expressed in many of the republics of the Caribbean, their efforts to add to their white elements in this way have not, in the main, been crowned with success, outside the case of Cuba. A small number of Germans, attracted by the prospects of the coffee culture, are to be found in Guatemala; a small colony of European Jews has recently settled in the Dominican Republic; there are sprinklings of European elements to be found elsewhere; but nowhere has there been a truly important movement. Even under the favorable circumstances of the first part of the century, when governments commonly opposed no or very few obstacles to the departure of some of their citizens to another land, there was no great enthusiasm for the Caribbean states; and in the much more difficult and complex conditions of the present day the chances of recruiting large numbers of immigrants are still less. We may safely assume, therefore, so far as we can see ahead, that the populations of the Caribbean will grow by natural increase rather than by accretion from abroad; that they will maintain their somewhat mixed character in most of the states concerned; and that they will continue to reflect much the same cultural influences that have helped to form them in the past.

There is, however, one fundamental question that has to be discussed in connection with Caribbean populations, a question fundamental, indeed, for society in general, and that is the relationship of the inhabitants of these various states to the areas they inhabit.

The density of population in a given country bears always a significant, though by no means a constant, relationship to the possibilities of economic progress. It is obvious that a highly industrialized area can support more persons than a purely agricultural one; it is obvious that an area fortunately situated with regard to the routes of trade, and in easy communication with the rest of the world, is better situated than one extremely remote; it is obvious that a country in which the habit of industry, and the desire of economic self-improvement is keen can make a better go of its economic life than a country in which large numbers of the inhabitants are devoid of any very profound urge to action, and are content with a relatively low standard of living. There is not, and cannot be, therefore, any rule of thumb by which it can be established in a given case whether this or that region is underpopulated or overpopulated; yet underpopulation and overpopulation nonetheless bear a fundamental relationship to the whole question of economic growth. This matter, indeed, often receives in American thought less attention than it deserves; and for that reason we ought to consider it with care.

But, first of all, a word more on the side of generalization. It is clear, for example, that in a given area there may dwell a number of people utterly inadequate to the exploitation of the natural resources of that area; and in such a case there cannot be rapid economic growth. More important, however, there may be in a given area a population larger than that area can comfortably support, and which is growing at a rate which makes economic progress difficult. In a poor country, with a high birth rate, the increase in numbers may be greater than the increase in the means of subsistence; and as a result of such a process the masses may be condemned to something very like permanent poverty. This is by no means merely a theoretical possibility; it is, in all probability, the situation which actually exists in some important parts of the world today. In China, for example, there is a very rapid increase in population; and this increase does in actual practice make a rise in the standard of living extremely difficult. In the case of China, something could be gained, it is true, if the land of the country were taken out of the hands of the great landed proprietors, who exploit the Chinese masses and keep them in a state of semi-peonage, and distributed among the people; but one of the most careful and thoughtful of analysts of China during the last few years has expressed it as his opinion that even if agrarian reform were carried to its ultimate goal, there would still remain a problem of overpopulation which nothing but drastic measures could possibly solve. This is, indeed, a dreary view to take, and the natural optimism of the American mind reacts against it, but nevertheless it may very possibly be true.

The same considerations might well apply to India. Despite the increasing industrialization of the country, which, of course, makes possible the support of a larger and larger number of people, many of our best students of population believe that in India the rate of natural increase is greater than the increase in the available means of subsistence; and on such a basis they reluctantly predicate a most unhappy future for the people of that enormous land. It is well, of course, not to be too dogmatic in such matters; but it is also well not to reject, from some kind of blind cheerfulness, what may be a very important matter to understand. And it is necessary, moreover, in connection with this question of possible overpopulation, to face one other unpleasant, but inescapable, fact; the fact that our modern health measures, in circumstances such as those which we have just depicted, may operate to complicate, rather than to alleviate, the economic problems of such areas as we have been describing. Decreases in infant mortality, and improvement in the physical well-being of adults, can have only a good effect in countries which are in process of development, and in which the numbers of the people bear some reasonable relation to the resources to be developed; but they can have a very different effect if a country is struggling with a difficult problem owing to its restricted area and its redundant population. Certainly, it is a most important question to decide in connection with any part of the world as to whether the general tendencies with regard to population are such as to encourage hope for the future, or such as to lead to a justifiable pessimism. Let us look, then, at the republics of the Caribbean from this point of view.

The general picture which confronts us is by no means a depressing one. In the states of Central America there is only one which can be regarded as already maintaining a very considerable population in a restricted area. This state is El Salvador. The whole area of the country is only about 10,000 square miles, approximately the size of Vermont. As compared with Vermont, with a population of something like 300,000, this little Caribbean state supports something like one million eight hundred thousand persons, or 183 persons per square mile. This is not so high a population density as that of many industrial countries, and it is not so high as many of the islands of the West Indies; but it is two and one-half times as great as that of any other of the Central American republics. In considering this figure, of course, we must take account of the general character of the area, and in particular we must ask ourselves the question as to whether there is any likelihood of a steadily increasing measure of industrialization. In the case of El Salvador, the country must be regarded as mountainous, and a very large extent of the area which can be cleared for cultivation has already been so developed. There are few signs of any industrial resources of an important character, and, therefore, very little chance that industrial development will take place on a considerable scale. In addition to these facts, it is to be noted that the birth rate in this little republic is high. All these facts taken together do not mean that at the present moment the situation is a desperate one, or that the absolute limit of healthy population growth has been attained. We must always make allowances, moreover, for improved methods of cultivation, for the change in agricultural habits from an export crop, in this case, coffee, to products that can be domestically consumed, and for declining rates of population increase as the pressure becomes more severe. One of the most distinguished students of Latin-American geography, in considering the future of El Salvador, is not disposed to take too pessimistic a view. Nonetheless, it would not be realistic to fail to recognize that there is here a developing problem, and that the coming years may increase the economic difficulties of what is today one of the most attractive and energetic communities of the Caribbean area.

With regard to the other Central American states, there is certainly no immediate problem. Figures of population density, it is true, do not tell the whole story, if based upon the total area of the state; we should only have an accurate measure of the future if we knew precisely how large a part of the whole were cultivable, and unfortunately accurate statistics for an answer to this question do not exist; but even the rougher figures that it is possible to assemble make it certain that there is a very substantial possibility of development in the other five republics of the region. The figures themselves are as follows: for Guatemala a population of 70 to the square mile, for Honduras a population density of only 22, for Nicaragua a population density of 22, for Costa Rica of 27, and for Panama of under 20. These statistics wear a little different aspect if, in addition to them, we examine the birth rates, and particularly the excess of births over deaths. We may take both the gross and net birth rates, and for purposes of comparison we may also note the similar rates in the United States. The gross figures are as follows: for Guatemala, 45.6, for Honduras, 39, for Nicaragua, 33.2 (for Managua only), for Costa Rica, 46, and for Panama, 27.3, for the United States, 17. The net rates, that is, the excess of births over deaths, are as follows: for Guatemala, 24, for Honduras, 21.6, for Nicaragua, 17.1, for Costa Rica, 23.1, for Panama, 16, for the United States, 6.1. It is obvious, therefore, that population increase is taking place in all these republics at a rate far greater than it is in this country. But even when this fact is taken into account, even when due allowance is made for the substantial amount of non-cultivable areas in many of these states, for the jungles of Panama, or the barren wastes of northern Guatemala, to cite only two examples, it is still fairly obvious that it will be quite a while before any acute problem of population pressure arises. On the contrary, if conditions are in general even moderately favorable, the increase of population that is taking place will have a tonic effect upon the national economies. With wise policies of internal development, with the proper external assistance, it may be hoped that the states of Central America will play a far more important role in the future than they have played in the past.

What is true of Central America is true, in a measure, of the island states of Cuba and the Dominican Republic. The density of population in neither of these states suggests that they are reaching the saturation point; and while as in the case of the Central American republics both the gross and the net birth rate is high, it does not threaten to bring about a really dangerous situation for some time to come.

When we come to Haiti, however, we are confronted by a very different situation. Here, in fact, is the most densely populated independent state of the New World. Within an area of about 10,000 square miles, an area hardly more than the state of Vermont (to choose once again the illustration suggested for El Salvador), is concentrated a population of something like 3,000,000, or nearly 300 persons to the square mile. This is an even more striking example of overpopulation than India or China, and its only parallels occur in some of the other islands of the Caribbean. Professor Leyburn has graphically described the problem in his interesting work on the black republic.* "To grasp the import of Haiti's problem of overpopulation," he writes, "one should imagine the number of Vermonters sextupled, working with hand tools and using methods which their great-grandfathers would have considered antiquated; imagine the state with only a hundred miles of paved road, with no harnessed water power, no substantial fortunes, no middle class; imagine the farms gullied and worn out; ninety-five per cent of the people illiterate and undernourished; the state having no industry and practically no goods imported from New York, Massachusetts, or any other part of the United States. Under such conditions the low standard of living would be understandable.

"Haiti might also be compared with Mississippi. Less than a quarter the size of that American state, it nevertheless has a larger population. Both Haiti and Mississippi are agricultural, with few towns, although no part of Haiti now has land as richly fertile as that of the Yazoo Delta. The low standard of living of the Mississippi share-cropper, whether Negro or white, is notorious—yet he has access to a few of the perquisites of civilization, whether these be elementary schools or moving pictures; the Haitian peasant lacks even these. In America the undercurrent of feeling is that something should be, probably eventually will be, done to improve the lot of the share-cropper. Certainly there is wealth enough in the country at large to alleviate conditions where they are deemed to be socially unhealthy.

* James G. Leyburn, *The Haitian People* (New Haven: Yale University Press, 1941), pp. 269, 270.

Not so in Haiti; the land is poorer, the numbers even greater, the area much smaller; and there is no wealth in the country, nor enough social vision among the upper classes to deal with the relentless increase of numbers."

This picture, depressing as it is, can hardly be said to be much overdrawn; and the worst of the matter is that it is difficult to devise a remedy for conditions which every humane person must recognize as appalling.

The easy answer, for many Americans, to a situation of this kind, would be birth control; but in reality such measures are entirely impracticable. The population of the republic has not yet reached that point of culture where it can readily accept or apply artificial restraints to the process of reproduction; a great campaign of education can hardly be waged in a country where the standard of literacy is pitifully low; and the influence of the Church (Haiti is a Catholic country) would, in all probability be cast into the balance on the other side. The plain fact of the matter is that in Haiti, as in other countries where the problem of redundant population is most acute, there is the least chance of any effective measures being taken to meet the problem head on. If there is any hope at all of dealing with it, it most certainly does not lie in the direction we have been discussing.

Another answer that seems in theory a little more reasonable is migration. Haitians are not averse to attempting to improve their economic status by such means. Many of them indeed have actually tried to do so. But they have met with all kinds of obstacles. In the early thirties, for example, there took place a very substantial emigration of Haitians to the island of Cuba, where they found employment in the sugar fields. But it was not long before Cuban opinion reacted against this influx of foreign labor, and the Batista regime took prompt, vigorous, and indeed ruthless measures to compel the immigrants to return to their own country. And this in the face of the fact that we have already noted, that there is a considerable black population in Cuba, and there is probably less racial prejudice there than in any part of the Caribbean area.

Haitians have also made attempts to seep over the border into the much more thinly populated Dominican Republic. Here, too, however, despite the presence of a very substantial population of Negro blood, they have not been welcome. Indeed, in connection with this movement of migration, there occurred one of the great tragedies of the Caribbean area only a few years ago. There were in 1937 an estimated 60,000 Haitians living across the border. At governmental instigation, there suddenly broke out a movement of mass murder of these innocent people. At least five thousand were either butchered or drowned, and it is likely that three or four times this number actually met their death. The episode, indeed, caused a little international crisis in the island of Santo Domingo. The government of President Trujillo was roundly accused by the authorities at Port-au-Prince of complicity in this outrage. A committee of the United States, Mexico, and Cuba investigated, and awarded Haiti damages of $750,000, a third of which was paid at once, and the rest promised in installments. But pecuniary compensation could not, after all, restore life, nor does it alter the fact that the Dominican Republic is resolved to prevent any very considerable movement of population from its neighbor state into its own area.

A third expedient for dealing with the evils of a redundant population is, of course, industrialization. The word may well be used in this connection in its widest sense, to include, that is, a highly organized agriculture, as well as manufacturing. But here again the prospects for the Negro republic do not look particularly bright. For one thing, Haiti lacks the material basis for the development of an industrial economy. It has no coal, no iron, and no oil.

There have recently been discovered small deposits of bauxite, and these may prove to be increasingly important, but they cannot, of course, serve as the basis of anything more than a single small industry. On the agricultural side, it may be possible to encourage the entry of American capital (a matter which we shall have to discuss again at a later stage in this volume), and thus to give a certain amount of employment to more and more Haitians. But the larger part of the profits of such enterprises are themselves exported, and the gain to the Haitian people is very far from striking.

Perhaps the greatest possibility of improvement lies in the development of better agricultural technique with regard to subsistence crops, which enter directly into the Haitian's standard of living. But even here progress must be slow, and must, of course, be dependent upon the diffusion of knowledge among the masses, a slow and laborious process in such a country as we are considering, and one that, unfortunately, is not regarded with much enthusiasm by the small governing class. When, therefore, one takes all the facts into consideration, it is not easy to be extravagantly cheerful about the future of the black republic.

But Haiti is not the only part of the Caribbean where the problem of overpopulation raises its head. The American colony of Puerto Rico is another example of the dangers that lie in human fecundity, and in a very high birth rate. We do not need here to analyze the matter in detail, and perhaps it ought to be said that a highly aggravating circumstance in this little island is the monopolization of much of the best land by sugar culture and the actual decline in the number of small peasant holdings that has taken place in the forty odd years since the Spanish-American War. But the peril of such a situation is that the social discontent which it provokes may easily spread to other parts of the Caribbean; and from this point of view it is not

possible entirely to ignore what is happening in the colonial
or semi-colonial areas of the whole region.

The British, too, have had to face this problem in the
populous Negro islands which lie to the south of Haiti and
of Puerto Rico. Barbados, for example, is one of the most
densely populated places in any part of the world. Jamaica
is another. And the population question undoubtedly helps
to explain in no small degree the unrest which took place
in Britain's colonial possessions in the Caribbean in the years
just preceding the outbreak of World War II. Matters
reached a very serious pass by the year 1938, and a British
Royal Commission was appointed to investigate the situation
and to make a report. This report dealt more lightly than
the facts justified with the problem of increasing population pressure, but its recommendations were nonetheless
directly related to the necessity of developing the subsistence industries, and raising the colonial standard of living.

We have now analyzed in some detail the population
problems of the area of the Caribbean. What general conclusions can we draw at the close of this chapter? Shall the
judgment be a pessimistic or an optimistic one?

It will be neither. It will be a balanced one. Where redundant population exists, it is impossible to be overly hopeful,
though even here improved agricultural methods, and perhaps the very pressure of the birth rate itself, may operate
to relieve the situation. We shall have to recognize, on the
less cheerful side, that there are in some of the states substantial populations that are in that primitive stage of economic development where their desire for self-improvement
is very limited, and their wants very few. Such, of course,
is the situation of the Haitian peasant, of the Guatemalan
Indian, and of other groups who have been given mention.
But, in the main, there are large areas which may undergo
a measure of healthy growth. The island of Cuba, as we
shall see, may well have a brilliant future. Much of Central

America possesses very positive assets, and ought to go forward to a far greater degree of prosperity than it enjoys today. The Dominican Republic is capable of much improvement. The peoples of these various states are by no means lifeless and inert, or without that urge to positive accomplishment which is the best guarantee of accomplishment itself. There are problems, on the economic, as on the human side. We must examine them as we proceed. But we do not need, we ought not, begin this study in any atmosphere of pessimism. We can, with the reservations already made, and with clear understanding of others in the economic sphere that must be made, legitimately hope for an expanding economy in much of the area of the Caribbean, and the progressive amelioration of the social conditions that exist there.

2. The Economic Background

The problems of the modern world are to a large extent economic. They are also of formidable complexity. They are certainly not to be solved by clichés. It is easy to bandy about such terms as "communism," and "free enterprise," and very difficult really to understand what is going on in the various states in the world. Terms such as those to which we have just alluded rarely tell the important part of the story. At all times in human history societies have differed from one another in their economic organization, in their political ideals, and in their cultures. Feudalism was characteristic of the middle ages, but the feudal system of France was not the same as that of Britain or of Italy. Mercantilism was characteristic of the sixteenth and seventeenth centuries, but it was not the same in its actual operation in England and in Spain. Capitalism is a convenient term to describe the economic order of the nineteenth century, but it did not operate in just the same way at any given moment in any two economies. The regulated or semi-regulated economic order into which the world is now moving will not be the same in any two countries, if it is looked at in detail, rather than superficially. Catchwords do little to clarify the situation; only analysis can make comprehensible what is actually going on.

From this point of view, it is far more important to understand the actual conditions in the Caribbean than it is to state that the economic system which exists there is a capitalistic order. The underlying realities in the situation are the following: (1) that the Caribbean states are agricultural and will for a long time remain preponderantly agricultural; (2) that they have been to an unfortunate degree developed on a monocultural basis, of dependence on one, or at most two or three, great staples; (3) that capital accumulation does not take place in most of them on a scale sufficient to ensure their healthy growth; (4) that they depend to a substantial degree on exports for the funds necessary to promote internal progress; (5) that they are, because of all these facts, very dependent upon the working of the world economy as a whole, and likely to undergo favorable or unfavorable conditions precisely as the great centers of economic life enjoy them; (6) that the future of these communities depends upon outside capital, public or private; (7) that the fixing of a sound relationship between the great capital-exporting nations and these communities is one of the most critical problems of the future. Of these seven generalizations the last may be properly expanded when we come to discuss the relations of the United States with the Caribbean states; but the other six deserve to be considered here.

The contrast between the agricultural and the industrial order in the modern world is one which goes deep to the roots of organized society. Everywhere, where the standard of living is highest, there has been a significant development of manufactures and of industry; indeed, the industrial process has been in a large part of the world the distinctive process by which a higher standard of living has been attained. Industrialization, moreover, stimulates and is accompanied by the spirit of social change; and industrial states, whether conservative Americans like it or not, are inevitably moving, where they have attained the greatest strength, towards wider and wider measures of control by government. In saying this, it is not to be thought that the same tendencies have not occurred in agricultural communities;

but it is, on the other hand, true that states where the mass of the people are still close to the soil are far less likely to undergo radical transformation in their economic order, and far less likely to succeed in attaining the same measure of internal prosperity, than their industrial rivals. Not only the degree of economic progress but the context in which it takes place is to some degree determined by the balance of agricultural and industrial life. In Great Britain of today, for example, the fact that the economy is overwhelmingly industrial has not only led to the growth of a party based upon the organization of labor, but it has made possible the widespread acceptance of measures of social control; in the United States, on the other hand, the presence of large rural elements, and their great importance in the scheme of politics, makes the growth of a Labor party, in the literal sense, more difficult, and also creates a different attitude with regard to regimentation.

These generalizations are of great importance for our subject. For the republics whose economic life we are analyzing have been preponderantly rural in character. This is not to say that the balance which tips so heavily in favor of agriculture today will not in the future be somewhat less heavily inclined on that side; but it is to say that by far the greater part of the population of the nine republics we are to examine will, for a long time to come, continue to make their living from the soil.

The reasons for this are not far to seek. Industrialization, in the full sense of the word, depends upon the presence in a given country of the key raw materials which make the wheels of industry hum. These are coal, iron, and oil. There are very limited sources of all three of the raw materials just mentioned in the area we are considering. In the Central American republics, for example, there is no iron, no oil, and no coal on a scale worth considering. The same thing applies to Haiti and to the Dominican Republic. Cuba is not in precisely the same position. Of the iron resources of Latin America, amounting to about 12,000,000,000 tons of high-grade deposits, Cuba has about one-fourth. Obviously, this is a fact of significance. But she does not possess important quantities of either of the staple fuels, and she must depend, therefore, upon her hydroelectric energy to carry out any policy of expansion on a grand scale. In her case, there is reason to think that progress will be made, but hardly such as to make it possible to predict that in any foreseeable future she will be a great industrial power.

Of course, in attempting to generalize about the Caribbean economies we must take into account light industry, and mining, as well as heavy industry, in making the contrast with agriculture. There is likely to be a modest development along these lines in more than one of the republics with which we are concerned. In the Central American countries, for example, there are beginnings in the milling of wheat, in the making of lard, in brewing, and even in the manufacture of cotton goods, to take only a few examples. In the Dominican Republic there is a small packing industry, at least one large cigarette factory, and a beginning is being made in textiles. And in Cuba there has been a really considerable development in cigar manufacture, in the shoe industry, and a whole variety of smaller enterprises in the field of textiles, paper, and metal working.

In addition to all this, there is in the Caribbean area a certain amount of mining. Cuba, as we have already seen, has an important iron industry. She has, too, a manganese industry in the province of Oriente, and this has made much progress since 1936, especially under the favoring influence of our liberal tariff arrangements with the republic. In Haiti there are said to be deposits of bauxite, though these have not yet been worked on any important scale. In the Central American countries there is a certain amount of the precious metals. There is, for example, a large silver mine in Honduras, which, though it has been worked for years, is still yielding silver on an important scale. Nicaragua has had a boom in the production of gold within the last decade. Small quantities of other minerals, chromium and antimony in Guatemala, manganese in Costa Rica, have been produced, and on an increasing scale in the years of war.

But all these developments taken together do not alter the fundamental fact to which we have already alluded; the countries of the Caribbean are and will remain agricultural.

To say, however, that a given state is preponderantly agricultural in its nature, without going a step further, is hardly an adequate description of its economic organization. It is important to know *how* the agricultural life of the state is organized, whether on the basis of numerous small freeholdings, or on the basis of great estates; and whether there is a tendency towards the growth of one or the other of these two types of rural economy. Obviously, the existence of great concentrations of land in the hands of a few suggests a pattern in some degree derived from the past; critical people would describe it as feudal; and under the conditions and in the social atmosphere which exists in the world today, the question would naturally arise whether such concentrations could continue to exist, or whether there would not be an increasing popular resentment against them. What are the facts from this point of view with regard to the area of the Caribbean?

In some parts of the region we are examining, there can hardly be said to be any organization at all. The Haitian peasant, for example, has simply squatted on the land; he may have, indeed does have, some primitive sense of ownership; but he certainly does not have any idea of what constitutes a title; he is not likely to change. In the same way, in the parts of Guatemala most populated by Indians, there has not been and is not likely to be any *system* of land-holding; the easiest thing to do with the heirs of the Mayas is to let them go their own way, and not try to force them into a mold that is alien to their thoughts and traditions. What happens among the San Blas Indians, or the inhabitants of the Isthmus of Darien, is equally irrelevant to the general question that we are here considering.

Leaving these people aside, as we may fairly do, it is next to be observed that there is at least one of the states in which we are interested where the small farmer is the typical figure. That state is Costa Rica. In 1938, in this remarkable little country of only about 700,000 people, more than two-thirds of the heads of families were landowners. The exact proportions were 71.7 per cent. Costa Rica, however, stands alone. In no other Caribbean country is there anything like so wide a diffusion of landownership.

Take, for example, the situation in Cuba. There the number of small landholders is less than it was when Cuba was a colony of Spain. There were, in 1899, 60,711 farms in the new republic. But by 1935 the number had shrunk to 38,105, despite the increase in the population. By a still later reckoning it has been calculated that only about an eighth of the land of the island is in the hands of small farmers, while more than a quarter is in the hands of great proprietors, native or foreign.

Or, from Cuba, let us turn for a moment to Guatemala. There our statistical information is not so accurate or satisfactory. But it would appear from the admirable study of Professor Chester Lloyd Jones * that large landholders held in 1940 about a third of the cultivated land of the country. In other words, there was a heavy concentration of property in a relatively small group. The total situation led distinctly to the conclusion that the great estate, rather than the small farm, was the typical form of landed property held in full title.

It is not perhaps necessary, and from the statistical point

* *The Caribbean Since 1900* (New York, 1936).

of view it might be impossible, to analyze the situation in all the other states. There are *some* small landholders in all of them, no doubt. In the Dominican Republic, for example, there is a considerable number of these people in the region known as the Cibao. There is a substantial proportion of relatively small holders in such a state as Salvador. In Honduras and Nicaragua the situation is less favorable, but we cannot say that no little proprietors exist. But nowhere is the situation what one would like to find it; nowhere does it conduce to the development of the soundest economic basis for the life of the people.

To say this, however, is not to say that there is today, broadly speaking, such an agrarian problem in any part of the Caribbean as there is in Mexico. Great landed estates can cause serious social troubles; the whole tendency of the times is towards their breakup, as can be readily seen from the history of Eastern Europe; but the intensity with which this need is felt will vary with the character of the people, and also with the pressure of population growth. The latter factor, we have already seen, while it applies to some of the islands, does not apply, at least in the same degree, to the mainland states we have been studying, with the possible exception of El Salvador; and the state of political consciousness among the masses is not yet such in any one of them, except Cuba, as to lead us to believe that agrarian unrest will appear on an important scale in the immediate future, or at any rate that it will attain such proportions as it did in Mexico after the Revolution of 1910.

There is, however, one factor that is of great importance and that will undoubtedly influence the character of the problem in the future. In many of the republics the great concentrations of land of which we have been speaking are in the hands of foreigners. This is the case in Cuba, where the great sugar properties (of which more anon) are largely in the hands of Americans. It has also been the case in Guatemala, until the recent war, where Germans held large amounts of land devoted to coffee culture, and where American interests, especially in the coastal regions, are of great significance. It is the case in such states as Nicaragua and Honduras, where large areas have been taken up by the great fruit companies. It hardly needs to be said that, in these days of intense national feeling, the absorption of a large part of the resources of the state by aliens creates a delicate and difficult situation, all the more so since some of the lands that are held are not in actual use for the growing of crops. The hostility with which such developments are viewed may be mitigated by various factors, such as the absence of intense population pressure; but that it should always be latent, and that it should sometimes be expressed, is not strange, and suggests that there is a difficult problem of international relations ahead.

But the distribution of the agricultural land calls attention to another aspect of the general economic situation in the Caribbean which is of very profound importance. As we have already said, the distinctive feature of Caribbean agriculture is its dependence upon a few great staples, of which the most important are sugar, coffee, and fruit. If we take the statistics of general agricultural production in some of these states, the situation, as seen in the first instance, may not appear so unhappy; for there is a substantial amount of subsistence agriculture. In Guatemala, for example, the corn crop far exceeds in amount the amount of one of the crops to which we have alluded. But if we have regard to exports (and exports as we shall later see are of transcendent importance in the Caribbean economy), the situation is far less cheering. The table at the top of page 42 will illustrate the situation.

Putting the matter another way, three of the republics out of nine were, in the year specified, dependent upon a single crop for three-quarters or more of their export

Country	Major exports, in percentages			Year
Costa Rica	Coffee, 49%	Bananas, 28%	Cacao beans, 85%	1938
Cuba	Sugar, 79%	Tobacco, 10%		1938
Dominican Republic	Sugar, 65%	Cacao, 13%	Coffee, 10%	Pre-war average
El Salvador	Coffee, 87%	Gold and silver, 6%		1938
Guatemala	Coffee, 65%	Bananas, 25%	Chicle, 5%	1938
Haiti	Coffee, 50%	Cotton, 15%	Sugar, 11%	1938
Honduras	Bananas, 62%	Gold and silver, 23%		1941–42
Nicaragua	Gold, 42%	Coffee, 32%	Bananas, 8%	1939
Panama	Bananas, 74%	Cacao, 12%		

trade; five more were dependent upon a single crop for more than half, or practically half, of their export trade; and, in the case of the one remaining, the principal export accounted for 42 per cent of the whole. Or, stating the matter in other terms, in five of the states two exports accounted for more than 80 per cent of the whole; in three more two exports accounted for more than 70 per cent; and in the one remaining two exports accounted for 65 per cent. There could hardly be more striking illustrations of the generalization which we are discussing.

Nor is this all. In considering the situation in the Caribbean states, we must take account of several other facts. In the first place, it ought to be pointed out that these states are by no means the only sources of the raw materials that bulk so large in the above table. As is well known, for example, coffee is produced on a very large scale in Brazil, to mention only the greatest of numerous competitors. Sugar is produced in many other areas, and in addition there is an important beet-sugar industry, which has to be taken into consideration. As for bananas, the West Indian Islands come into competition with the independent republics of the region, and there is no reason why the production of bananas should not be carried on an increasing scale in many other tropical regions.

In no sense of the word, then, can the Caribbean states be said to enjoy a monopoly position in their distinctive fields of agricultural production. Moreover, and the fact is highly important, there is not for any foodstuff an indefinitely expansible market. This is not to say that the consumption of sugar, or coffee, or bananas has necessarily reached its peak. Predictions of this kind are extremely dangerous. But it is to say that one cannot be entirely sure of a favorable market situation and of a constantly growing demand over a long period of time. The development of the world economy as a whole will no doubt determine the degree to which nations engaged in the production of the great staples are able to prosper in the future. But, putting the matter bluntly, and stating a fact that may be displeasing to the national pride of some of the countries whose economic position we are considering, the Caribbean economies are *dependent* economies, and nothing in the world can alter this fundamental fact for some time to come.

Perhaps it would be illuminating in this regard to go a step further. They are, it has just been said, dependent on the world economy, and that is true. But they are particularly dependent upon the economy of the United States, and increasingly so, it would appear, as time goes on. The following table will help to make the situation clear.

Percentage of imports sent to the U. S.

Country	1913	1938	Country	1913	1938
Cuba	79.9	76.0	Guatemala	27.2	70.7
Dominican Rep.	53.5	32.1	Honduras	86.9	90.7
Haiti	8.8	42.8	Nicaragua	35.3	77.5
Costa Rica	50.8	45.6	Panama	89.2	89.2
El Salvador	28.4	61.7	Average	48.8	64.0

The years that have been selected for analysis in the above table are years when the statistics are not distorted by war, or by such abnormal conditions as the great boom of the late twenties. If scrutinized closely, they show that with three exceptions, Cuba, the Dominican Republic, and Costa Rica, all of the Caribbean states increased their dependence upon the United States in the quarter of a century between 1913 and 1938; that in two of the other three cases the situation was not materially changed, and that in only one was there a significant decline in the percentage of imports sent to this country. When we say, therefore, that the well-being of our southern neighbors is vitally connected with our own, we are simply stating a more and more obvious fact. A depression in our own economy will inevitably communicate itself to these other communities. And the significance of this fact will become still more evident when, in later pages, we come to consider our foreign policy in its economic implications, and the problems of maintaining that expanding economy of which the whole world stands in need.

There is another way in which the situation of the Caribbean countries can be made clearer. The existence of a monocultural, or at least of a largely monocultural economy, the dependence upon foreign markets for the sale of the product, and the obvious impossibility of these small states controlling the general trend of the world economy means that they are subjected to serious price oscillations with regard to their principal staples. The most dramatic illustration of how very serious the situation may become is afforded by the experience of the Cuban sugar industry during the years immediately following World War I. During the war years the United States persuaded the Cuban Government to accept a fixed price for its sugar, 4.60 cents in 1917 and 5.50 in 1918. These prices were sufficiently high to augment production considerably, and to lead to the development of new mills. With the end of the conflict the controls were ended, and there ensued a period of wild speculation, to the extent that in the spring of 1920 sugar had gone to the fantastic price of 22½ cents. Then came the inevitable reaction. From May 19, 1920, the price of sugar began to slip, first slowly, then more and more rapidly, and, by the 13th of December, it had reached the ruinously low figure of 3¾ cents. Many Cuban sugar planters were ruined; many Cuban sugar estates passed into the hands of New York banks; and at a distance of more than twenty years Cubans still speak mournfully of the experience of 1920 as "the dance of the millions." The history of the subsequent years illustrates in the same way the dangers and difficulties involved in the price structure of a staple. During the twenties, after the initial upset, sugar prices began to improve. Sugar-beet areas in Europe had not been restored to their former yields, and world consumption was increasing. By 1923 sugar had reached a price of 6 cents a pound. Once again expansion took place, and once again the price began to fall, going as low as 2 cents by 1925. A temporary improvement then took place, and by 1927 the price was four cents. But this relative prosperity did not last long. A new descent began, and by 1929 the situation was already serious. Then came the Great Depression. Sugar plummeted downward to virtually unprecedented levels. It was never above two cents in the depression years, and at the worst, in 1932, it had reached sixty hundredths of a cent a pound.

In view of the problem created by shifting prices, the Cuban government has during the last twenty years tried various expedients to deal with the situation. For example, when prices began to fall in the years following 1923, the Cuban sugar planters urged upon Congress and secured the adoption of a law aimed at a 10 per cent reduction of the crop. The next year this law was strengthened; and control was quite effectively exercised. In 1928 the same experiment was tried again. But reduction of acreage in a single country could hardly be expected to produce any useful results. Indeed, this first experiment in control of a crop that was marketed largely in a competitive export market has been well described by one authority as "futile, and almost naive." In 1928 the experiment was abandoned. For national control international control was substituted in the early thirties. After long negotiations, in which the Cuban government was none too considerately treated by the Oriental sugar producers, a convention was signed in 1931, fixing quotas for some of the principal sugar-producing regions. But once again difficulties of a serious nature arose. The plan proved far from easy to enforce; and the Brussels agreement, as it was called, only covered areas producing about 70 per cent of the sugar entering into international trade. There seemed to be no health in any such expedient, either.

With the coming of the New Deal more intelligent measures were taken, especially designed to give to Cuba a fair share of the American market, and these measures will be more properly considered in a later portion of this volume. By these means, more than by any others, it is possible to provide some degree of stability for the Cuban producer. But they depend (and we may have to revert to the fact later) on the situation in the United States, on the chances of American politics, on the wise reconciliation of sharply divergent interests. So long as Cuba is preponderantly a one-crop country, she is likely to have her troubles, and to be dependent to a highly undesirable degree upon the good will and intelligence of those who live beyond her borders.

What has been true of sugar, in the last twenty years, has also been true of coffee, the second great staple of the Caribbean area.

In November of 1914, for example, coffee was selling at

about six and one-quarter cents a pound. By June of 1919, it had reached twenty-five cents a pound. It then began a rapid descent, to fourteen cents by July of 1920, and to five cents by March of 1921. After this, recovery set in and reasonably good prices were obtained by the growers in the middle twenties. But the Great Depression produced another catastrophic decline. Between July 1929 and June 1930, the price fell from 16 and ⅜ to 7 and ¼ cents. From this collapse indeed the staple never recovered in the thirties, never getting up to as much as nine cents, and hitting in 1939 an all-time low of 4 and ⅛ cents a pound. The essential explanation of this disorganized situation in the industry lay, of course, in overproduction. In the thirties, Brazil, the greatest of producers, in a desperate effort to deal with the situation, resorted to the destruction of enormous supplies, the figure rising as high as 180,000,000 pounds in the year 1938–39. The war, however, brought a change in the situation. And, in addition, measures of international control were set up in 1941 which immensely improved the position of the coffee growers. With a reasonable degree of intelligence, and a little of the spirit of international coöperation, matters ought not again to come to quite the pass they reached less than a decade ago.

But it ought to be said that no system of control, and not even international measures which operate to stabilize the market, can really go to the heart of the problem of a monocultural economy. Such an economy is adjudged by many people today to be inherently undesirable, and there is a strong case for this point of view. For example, in the case of sugar, closely connected with dependence on this single crop, there is a seasonal dislocation that cannot be ignored. "From December to June," says Professor Chester Lloyd Jones, who has contributed immensely to the understanding of the Caribbean, "during the dry season, activity is at its height; there is a scarcity of labor; wages are, for the Caribbean region, very high; the whole country gives the impression of a factory run at high speed. Then comes the 'dead' season. Preparation for the next crop proceeds leisurely. There is a great deal of idleness or semi-idle-employment throughout the country. . . . Taking the year as a whole, the man-power of the republic is very unevenly and inefficiently used." * These comments go to the root of one aspect of the matter. Granted that it were possible to attain a far greater degree of stability than now exists, it would still seem to be unwise for any country to depend, to the degree that many of the republics of the Caribbean depend, upon one or two crops for the maintaining of their export trade, and the fundamental developments of their economic life.

For reasons such as these, a question that is highly apposite to the future development of the Caribbean countries is the degree to which they are capable of a greater degree of diversification than exists today. The healthiest economies are economies of variety. Is there an opportunity for the development of such economies in the republics we have been considering? To what degree have measures been taken, or are measures projected with this end in view?

The question has certainly not failed to be considered in the last twenty years, and perhaps the most ambitious practical program has been that of Cuba. As long as twenty years ago, in the presidency of Machado, steps were taken to widen the range of economic activities carried on on Cuban soil. By virtue of a protective duty, a great increase in coffee production took place, and Cuba has produced sufficient coffee since the beginning of the thirties to satisfy the greater part of her domestic consumption. The cultivation of corn has become more and more important. A cattle industry has grown up, and along with it a dairy industry. Poultry raising has been encouraged, and in this

* Chester Lloyd Jones, *Caribbean Backgrounds and Prospects.* (New York: D. Appleton & Co., 1931), p. 105.

field, too, much progress has been made. Of course, there are two sides to the question of stimulating, by protective tariffs, the growth of domestic industry. Such a policy, if not wisely conceived, may result in a very substantial increase in the cost of living, and may impose a heavy burden upon the masses through a rise in the price of the necessities. But, in some of the cases just mentioned, the infant-industry argument, that has always been the mainstay of the more rational advocates of protection, will undoubtedly apply. And beyond and above this, the point may be made that *some* increase in the price of *some* commodities may be a price worth paying for a better-balanced economy. Here at home, in the course of the last decade and a half, the people of the United States seem to have come close to committing themselves to a policy which amounts to the subsidization of agriculture. Such a policy can be defended in terms of the social health of the American community. It is the same way with measures of diversification in such a country as Cuba. The evils of monoculture are in many ways so great that there is a powerful argument for taking measures against it, even if these measures involve some sacrifice. It would need, in each case, a thorough examination of the facts over a fairly long term of years to discover whether in a given case these sacrifices were excessive.

In the other two island states of the Caribbean there are some signs of a broadening of the base of the economic life. In Haiti, which has been largely dependent upon coffee for the maintenance of its export trade, bananas are now appearing in the balance as well. Obviously, this is not so happy a development as if Haiti's second crop were one less competitive. But it is at least better than no second crop at all.

In the Dominican Republic the present ruler of the country, President Trujillo, has made something of an effort to diversify. By means of a heavy duty the production of corn has been much increased, and the Republic has been of

recent years a corn-exporting nation. In the decade of the
thirties, moreover, a substantial expansion took place in coffee culture. There was a less impressive expansion in the
growing of cacao, in which commodity this little state ranks
sixth among producing countries. The fly in the ointment
with regard to the Dominican situation is that the crops on
which most dependence is placed, outside of sugar, are precisely those which have a very bad price record in the past.
Here, again, any diversification may be regarded as better
than none, but we cannot say that the situation is a happy
one.

What is the situation with regard to Central America? Is
the rule of the coffee tree and banana tree likely to be
shaken? Are there other excellent possibilities for these little states? Here again the problem is being studied, and new
avenues of opportunity are opening up. For a long time past,
to cite one example, El Salvador has produced the misnamed,
and extremely important, balsam of Peru, useful in the treatment of disease. During the war an attempt has been made
to grow quinine in Guatemala, and, if this attempt is successful at all, it may well be of very great importance.
Abacá, or Manila hemp, which formerly came exclusively
from the Philippines, and which makes the strongest ropes
known, can be grown, and during the war has been grown,
in Central America. Rotenone, one of the most effective
insecticides, hitherto secured from the Orient, has during
the last few years been cultivated on an extensive scale in
Guatemala, Honduras, and Costa Rica, and chicle, the
basis of chewing gum, comes in great quantities from the
first of these countries as well as from Yucatán. It will not
do, however, to put too much faith in any of these possibilities; for not one of the products we have mentioned
(with the possible exception of chicle) is of a kind that
can be grown in Central America alone. All will in the
years ahead presumably come into competition with the

Orient. The Orient, indeed, will have an advantage in terms of cheap labor supply; whether this advantage will be more than balanced by nearness to the great markets and by better conditions of public order is something that no one ought to be bold enough to predict. We can only say that there is at least a possibility of development.

This is not the whole story, however. There are certainly parts of Central America, northern Honduras, for example, and El Salvador, where in course of time a cattle industry far more important than that which exists today might conceivably emerge. The corollary of the cattle industry, the dairy industry, might also grow with a rise in the standard of living, and with a general activation of the economy. The experience of Cuba, in short, might, with favoring circumstances, be reproduced, though not on the same scale, in the countries of the Isthmus. We ought not to paint the future in the glowing colors of a prospectus for a land sale, but there is reason to hope that the future may be one of gradual expansion and of broadening economic activity.

There is, however, one aspect of the problem of economic expansion and self-improvement that is of very great importance. There can be no adequate exploitation of the natural resources of any country where there do not exist adequate means of communication. The questions of railroads, of roads, and of air traffic are current matters of very real significance in the republics of the Caribbean.

No doubt the state which is best situated from this point of view is Cuba. Cuba has over 3300 miles of railway operated for public purposes, besides a great network of private lines. It possesses, too, a great Central Highway extending virtually from one end of the island to the other, and with a considerable number of spurs. From the point of view of road construction, however, there is still much that can be done. Indeed Cuba's total road mileage in 1941 was less than that of such smaller and poorer states as the Dominican Republic, El Salvador, Guatemala, and Nicaragua, not to mention others in South America.

The two republics of the island of Santo Domingo have benefited, so far as road building is concerned, from the period of the American occupation. Haiti was virtually roadless when the marines went in in 1915. Today it has a reasonably good system of paved roads, making it possible to travel to any part of the republic. The total mileage, it is true, is still small, the smallest of any Latin-American state, but this is not out of line with the general geographical facts of the situation, since the black republic is the smallest of all the independent countries of the Caribbean. As for the Dominican Republic, the road system there has undergone a great development since the American occupation. An important program was carried through during the period of control but succeeding governments have pressed forward, and President Trujillo has interested himself to an important degree in the extension of the highway system. Today the republic has 3180 miles of road, and approximately half of this has been built since 1929. The area along the northeast coast is now the only part of the country which cannot be reached by road, and this without regard to weather conditions. There is much work still to be done in opening up the mountain sections, but it is certainly safe to say that few other Caribbean states have made more progress in this field of activity than the Dominican Republic. In the circumstances an important railroad development is hardly needed, and has not taken place. There are privately owned sugar lines, and 152 miles of government line, but the latter seems destined to play a relatively small part in the developments of the future.

In the states of Central America the situation varies rather widely. Perhaps the state that is most meagerly equipped with means of communication is Honduras. Despite the fact that it is almost six times as large as Haiti, it actually has a smaller road mileage, and what exists is by no means all of it in first-class condition. There is a well-built and often-celebrated road that connects the capital, Tegucigalpa, with the west coast, but there are few other roads of similar construction. The government has during the war started another first-class road out of the capital towards the north coast, but as late as 1941 there were only 629 miles of improved road in the whole republic.

In Panama the situation is little better, if regard be taken for the country as a whole. There is, of course, a network of roads and railroads near the canal. But only a small part of the total area of the republic is served by highways, and large sections are not even mapped. The total road mileage, taking into account roads of all descriptions, is not one thousand miles.

In the other states of Central America the situation is somewhat better. The least well-situated is Nicaragua, where there are only one hundred miles of road, much of this far from suited to motor traffic; but in Nicaragua the deficiency is made up to some extent by the 171 miles of railway that tap the richest and most prosperous area of the republic. El Salvador has a very good system of national highways, no less than 1600 miles in extent, which is something of a record for a state only about 160 miles long and 60 miles wide. Guatemala has made immense progress under President Ubico, and by the close of 1941 possessed 3900 miles of road, some 400 of which were macadamized. Its central highways are today a pleasure to the tourist, as well as a boon to the man of business. And they are supplemented by a railway line which extends across the country from Puerto Barrios to the Pacific port of San José, a branch of which runs from the junction of Zacapa to the capital of El Salvador. Though the Guatemalans complain of the discrimination practiced by the railroad line (an affiliate of the United Fruit Company) with regard to the east coast ports, it would be hard to deny that International Railways, as it is called, has played a substantial part in the development of the country. Finally, Costa Rica shares with Guatemala the distinction of being the best provided with communications of any of the Central American states. In this little republic there are about 1800 miles of roads, and on the central plateau all the principal centers are linked by all-weather highways. In addition, there is a railway line from coast to coast, the first that was built in any part of the Isthmus, and one that has well served the Costa Rican economy for more than half a century.

It must not be supposed, however, that in any one of the Central American states the end of road building is in sight. Quite the contrary. Even in the more fortunate republics, such as Guatemala and Costa Rica, there is still much to be done, wide areas that can still come under development. And in addition to the necessity of opening up new regions, there is the great project of a Pan-American Highway, of which something must be said here. This grandiose idea, which looks eventually to the completion of a paved road which will extend from the southern boundary of the United States to the west coast of South America, and even beyond, has a long history. Construction upon it was started as much as nineteen years ago, and has been much accelerated by the war. The road now extends throughout the state of Guatemala, across the western strip of Honduras, and on through El Salvador. There are stretches of it in Nicaragua, in Costa Rica, and in Panama that remain to be completed, but the work goes on, and it is of very great importance. Such a road when finished will link the republics of Central America together, as they never have been before; it will probably open up in the long run a substantial tourist traffic; it will tap new areas; it will, to add a purely American consideration, contribute directly to the defense of the Canal. It represents, as we shall see, one of the most hopeful forms of coöperative action among American states, and one that benefits all.

Before leaving the subject of roads, there is one other aspect of the problem that is worth a word of mention. With roads, of course, must go vehicles to run upon them. The indices of motor travel for the Caribbean are well worth passing mention. In Haiti there were in 1944 only 2463 cars, for a population of 2,719,000. In the Dominican Republic there were 2463 cars for a population of about 2,000,000, or 1 in 800. The ratios for the other states are as follows: Cuba, 1 in 100, Costa Rica, 1 in 175, El Salvador, 1 in 475; Guatemala, 1 in 800; Honduras, 1 in 900; Nicaragua, 1 in 700; and Panama, 1 in 350. If these figures be compared with those of the United States, where in 1938 there was 1 vehicle to every 4 persons, they look pitifully small. And even if one takes the world average, said to be 48, they still underline the fact that the states of the Caribbean, for the most part, need not only roads, but vehicles to run on them. It is only in such a perspective that our figures with regard to highways can be seen in their true significance.

There is one form of transport that we have so far omitted to mention in our survey. That is, of course, the airplane, and it is important. In most of the Caribbean area the construction of highways is no light task. There are formidable topographical difficulties in many parts of Central America, where, as has been well observed, mountain, plain, valley, and jungle are all in close juxtaposition. The air-borne carrier meets under these conditions a special need. And it has been advancing to a more and more important place in the development of the whole region. There are today in Latin America almost as many miles of air lines as there are railway miles, and in only six of the twenty republics does railway mileage exceed airline mileage. In the Central American states, in fact, there was in 1943 more airline mileage per square mile of area than there was in the United States. Obviously, the airplane plays no such important role in the island republics, though Cuba is the center of a very important traffic. The expansion of air transport in the Caribbean suggests to the average American the highly-publicized and immensely powerful Pan-American Airways. There can be no doubt about the significance of this company's achievement. But less well known, and very important, is the company known as Taca, Transportes Aéreos Centro-Americanos, which has not only connected the capitals of the Isthmus but has also penetrated deep into the jungles, and which has 5600 miles of route, carries an immense amount of freight, and was, indeed, in 1944, the largest non-military carrier of freight in the world. To put the matter another way, and again to emphasize the full significance of this development in the five years 1937–1941, Taca carried from two and a half to nearly four times as much freight as all the domestic airlines of the United States combined. Perhaps the most dramatic form of its activity is the getting of chicle out of the jungle, where there are no roads, and where the white man can hardly penetrate in any other fashion than by air and comes in contact with Indians who have never even seen a train or an automobile. But it serves many other interests as well, and is certain to play an important role in the future development of Central America.

But neither roads, nor planes, nor railways, nor all put together, significant as each of them is, can guarantee the forward movement of the Caribbean states. Behind any of these there lies the need of capital, and of capital on a substantial scale. And the factors in this central problem must be analyzed here. In the first place, we must remember that these states are almost all of them poor. In the year 1944 the national income of the United States was $155 billion, or more than $1100 per capita. In no Caribbean states does it even remotely approach that figure. Estimates made by the Office of the Coördinator of Inter-American Affairs suggest the following: for Costa Rica, 95 million, for Cuba, 551, for the Dominican Republic, 100, for El Salvador, 103, for Guatemala, 303, for Haiti, 54, for Honduras, 68, for Nicaragua, 62, and for Panama, 45. On a per capita basis the best situated country is Costa Rica, with a figure of $134; at the other extreme is Haiti, where the figure is $20. It is obvious that the situation, from the angle of "saving" is very, very different from that which exists in the United States.

There is another central difficulty in the problem of capital formation in the Caribbean. Latin Americans are likely to be lavish spenders in good times; they are also likely, if they put money aside, to invest it in land, rather than in productive enterprise. Both of these characteristic forms of activity naturally hinder the accumulation of liquid capital; both make more difficult the process of economic growth. This is a fact of substantial importance; and since it has to do with deep-seated national habit, it seems hardly likely that it will rapidly change.

Wholly apart from these proclivities, however, we must understand that in the Caribbean "saving" does not play, and will not play for a long time to come, the decisive role in the formation of capital that it does in the United States or in some other advanced countries. Most economists agree that, in the great industrialized states, it is precisely this "saving" that determines to a substantial degree, perhaps to a decisive degree, the general course of the economy, and the ups and downs of the business cycle. But in such countries as those we have been examining, prosperity or adversity is more closely geared to the export trade. In the most favorable years large credits can, of course, be accumulated; some of these credits could be, and are, used for purposes of further expansion; but they are fully as likely, in the long run, to be spent abroad in providing some of the luxuries of life; and they afford, in any case, a very insecure basis for the necessary expansion of the economy.

Of course, there is another way to create capital besides

saving or export balances. This way is borrowing. In our own day, in advanced states, there is increasing support for this method of securing funds, especially in periods of depression. But in the Caribbean, historically speaking, there have been many difficulties in the way. Because of the small national income, the rate of interest in all Latin-American countries is, from the viewpoint of an American or an Englishman, extremely high; and governments, when they borrow abroad, have often had to borrow on what we would be likely to think of as extremely onerous terms. The history of many of these states, moreover, does not inspire, among foreign investors, an unlimited confidence in their ability to repay their loans. On the other hand, if recourse is had to the banks *within* the country some unpleasant consequences are likely to ensue. For as new money is created prices rise and the rate of interest increases. The rate at which this rise takes place is likely to be faster than it is in more highly industrialized countries where deficit financing, in times of distress, may put unemployed resources to work. The resulting inflation may bring acute distress, both political and social.

In any circumstances we may say, on the basis of the generalizations just made, that the problem of capital formation in the Caribbean will not be easy; and it is important to stress the fact that it can hardly take place without assistance from outside. This may, and often does, prove distasteful to the Latin American, but he must, if he be candid, admit the elementary fact. The terms of this borrowing, whether it shall be public or private, how it shall be regulated, and controlled, and many other cognate questions, will have to be discussed in later chapters when we turn to analyze the relations of the United States to the states of the Caribbean; but the broad general fact is one that must be stated here.

We ought not to close our survey of the economic situation in the Caribbean without examining more specifically for a little the relationship of the Caribbean economies to the war from which we have just emerged and to the peace that will follow it. Of the contribution of each one of them to the United States, and of the contribution of the United States to each, we shall take note in later pages. But it is worth while here to generalize about their situation, and to trace the broad effects of the outbreak of hostilities upon their way of life.

In the first place, since without exception these countries are raw material countries and since the demand for raw materials increases in war, the first effect of the struggle, it might be thought, was to activate their economies and to bring about a period of increasing prosperity. But this was true with qualifications that have to be taken into account. The coffee-producing countries, for example, lost the greater part of their European markets by virtue of the British blockade, and had to find their compensation in an expanding market in the United States. The fruit-producing areas in the Caribbean were hampered by a shipping shortage, by the drastic nature of the German submarine campaign in 1942, and by the low priorities which their products enjoyed in the nations which were engaged in conflict. The sugar-producing areas fared better, for by far the greater part of their output had, in the years before hostilities began, been taken by the United States and, in the case of the Dominican Republic, by Great Britain. After 1942, however, it is fair to say, the general trend was upward, and increasingly so as the war proceeded. Indeed, since in the war years exports exceeded imports, the states of the Caribbean area began to accumulate dollar balances which will stand them in good stead in the future. Undoubtedly, they have, in the broad sense, benefited from the events of 1941–1945.

But the benefit is by no means an unmitigated one. It seems reasonably clear, for example, that during the war period (and it would be safest not to press for accurate or even moderately satisfactory data beyond the end of the war), the Caribbean economies were less successful in dealing with the problems of inflation than was the United States. There were several reasons why this was so. In the first place, most of these countries were dependent upon imports for many of the products which they consumed, and imports were naturally restricted. It was impossible for them to buy freely and cheaply in the markets to which they were accustomed. In the second place, while some attempts at control were made, in general the countries with which we are concerned were less disposed to regulate than were the English-speaking states, and turned both to price control and to rationing with less speed and on a less important scale than did the United States.

In general, it may be said that, of all the countries with which we are concerned, the most successful in preventing unreasonable price rises were Panama and El Salvador, and the least successful were Nicaragua, Honduras, and Haiti. But our knowledge on these matters is by no means of the up-to-date kind which is possible in the case of the United States, and it is entirely possible, therefore, that the contemporary situation will have changed in substantial degree as compared with that of even eighteen months ago. For that matter, it has changed at home.

War inflation is, of course, an evil, and by this time it has been generally recognized as such. But it is less of an evil in simple economies than in complex ones. For one thing, there are large populations in some of the states of the Caribbean who can hardly be said to be geared to a pecuniary economy in any very conclusive way. The peasants of Haiti, the Indians of Guatemala, and other large groups living on what is substantially a subsistence economy, are not powerfully affected by the course of prices in more advanced communities. A large middle class, living on fixed incomes, and thus adversely affected by a rise in the cost of living, does not exist in most of the countries we have been studying. The impact of higher prices is felt, therefore, by a smaller group than in a more highly developed community. But this is not to say that the effects are negligible. Unrest connected with inflationary tendencies has certainly manifested itself in the Caribbean during the past years, and may well have contributed to the revolutions that took place in El Salvador and in Guatemala in 1944. It has undoubtedly been a factor, also, in the politics of Cuba.

On balance, to revert to the fundamentals of the economic situation, we may say that the Caribbean benefited economically from the war, but that there were qualifying circumstances that have to be taken into account. What will be its future in the first years of peace? How easily will it make the transition from one state to the other? What are the chances of serious unrest, and of serious dislocation?

Here, again, we must distinguish in the first place between a simple and a complex economy. The haunting peril that overhangs the great industrial states is the peril of unemployment. When Americans think of the future their minds go back to the thirteen million unemployed of 1932, and they ask themselves anxiously how such a catastrophe is to be avoided in the future. No other question is more central to the economic and political life of the great industrial state than this.

But the situation is very different in most of Latin America. It has been well stated by Professor Seymour Harris. "When depression strikes a Latin-American country," he writes, "the result is unlikely to be an increase in unemployment of the proportions which the United States and Great Britain can expect." Rather, the effect will be a small reduction of employment. But "the amount of unemployment or amount of employment changes relatively little, except in a fairly industrialized country like Argentina. To put the matter another way, the Caribbean worker is in most cases close to the soil; in so far as he forms a part of the world economy he is connected with forms of enterprise which do not, usually, shut down as factories shut down, the scale of his activities will be determined by the greater or less need for the products of his labor; but he will continue to subsist, in many instances, because of his own close contact with the land. The form which the social problem takes in such a case is somewhat different from that which it takes in more mature communities."

On the other hand it is not wise to minimize the effects of economic recession on the countries of the Caribbean. The wretchedness that spread through Cuba in the years of the Great Depression, the grave social and political situation that then resulted, the rise of dictatorial governments in a large part of Central America, and in the Dominican Republic, are testimony enough to the effect of the downswing of the economic pendulum. Obviously, it is important that these states should continue to be prosperous. And the point that needs to be emphasized in this connection is that they cannot be prosperous *alone*. They are (and perhaps the point has been made to the degree of tiresome iteration) dependent upon exports for their economic well-being. They can export only in an expanding economy, in a world that is developing and moving forward. Their problems are not national, but international. They must, therefore, command our fuller attention in that part of this book which is devoted to the analysis of their relations with the United States.

3. The Politics of the Caribbean

If we turn from economics to politics, what are the salient facts that we ought to understand with regard to the states of the Caribbean? In what respect are these states like our own? In what respects are they different? What are the prospects of American ideals and institutions coming more and more to be reflected in the life of these peoples with whom we are so closely associated?

Stated in the broadest terms, the answer to our question is not so very difficult to phrase. All of these states are republics, in the exact sense of the term; few of them are mature democracies, as we understand these words in the United States. Beyond this point generalization is difficult; and it will be impossible to deal with the questions we have just asked unless, in the course of this chapter, we subject each of the nine states of the Caribbean area to a separate and special analysis.

But first of all we can, lumping them together, say a word or two about the republican idea in the New World. The word "republican" may be simply defined; it is used by most of us in contradistinction to the word "monarchical" and it suggests a form of political organization in which, in theory at least, the power is derived from the people, and exercised by a chief executive who, in one form or another, is chosen by them. If we accept some such definition, we can say again that the countries which we have under examination are "republics." Haiti, indeed, which is the oldest of them as a national state, began as an Empire under a tough and ruthless despot whose name was Dessalines; after his death it split into two parts, one of which was governed by a king, the extraordinary Henri Christophe, whose immense citadel still towers over the plain of northern Haiti, and the other a republic, administered under the milder rule of a man named Pétion. But after 1820 the two parts of the country were united under President Boyer, and save for a new and brief monarchical experiment under a picturesque and illiterate savage whose name was Soulouque, it has been a republic ever since. You can still see Soulouque's crown in the vaults of National City Bank at Port-au-Prince, and an impressive piece of jewelry it is; but there is not the slightest reason to believe that there will be another Soulouque in the future. The monarchical idea, of course, is going out of fashion all over the world; only recently the ancient house of Savoy has been sent packing; even strongly reactionary states like Spain and Portugal do not seem to have much use for kings; and while there are still hereditary sovereigns left, there are not many instances in our days of a reversion to monarchical forms, unless the rather depressing case of Greece be cited as an example.

As for the seven states of the Caribbean which owe their origin to their revolt from Spain, there has been no important monarchical movement in any one of them since they first attained their independence. They are all of them at least a hundred years old, and in this respect their constitutions may well be considered as fixed. As for Panama, which came into being in 1903, there has been, of course, not a suggestion of any other than republican forms.

Now it may be thought that this matter of republicanism is so obvious that it need not be mentioned. But there is a little more to the matter than that. For what lies behind the republicanism of the states of the Caribbean is an aversion to hereditary power, to the institutionalizing of leadership in an individual raised above the mass, and separate from the mass; and this feeling, as we shall see a little later, operates to make more difficult than it would otherwise be the creation of totalitarian forms. Such forms, it is true, are not monarchical; but they are based upon respect for concentrated leadership; and where such respect does not exist they will find it more difficult to take root. This is a point to which we shall return; but it is just as well to state it at the beginning of this chapter.

When it comes to relating the history of these countries to our notions of democracy, however, the task is a little more difficult. What are the essentials of the ideal democratic state? What do we have in our minds when we think and talk of democracy as a method of government, as a means of organizing the life of the state? In the first place, we mean by democracy a government in which power is vested in the people. We cannot say that the suffrage must be absolutely coincident with the adult population; we would not exclude from our definition, for example, states in which the vote was still confined to men (though we might deprecate such a limited system) and we might even agree that certain special classes of people, possibly illiterates, might be excluded. New York State, for example, requires that all its citizens be able to read and write in order to vote, and we do not regard this requirement as undemocratic. But we cannot call a state a democracy unless the greater part of the people are entrusted with the franchise, and exercise that franchise under conditions of political freedom.

But it is not enough that the people are in theory entitled to participate in their own government; they must, certainly if they are to conform to the democratic ideal, exercise that privilege freely, and under conditions of good order. We would not call a state a democracy in which the voters, no matter how numerous, constantly voted under direction or under intimidation; or in which, after an election, it was common for the minority not to accept the decision of the majority; or in which the actual power was concentrated in the hands of a few persons, or exercised by a president who was all-powerful, once he had been elected. We would wish, too, to be reasonably sure that the forms of the democratic process were not merely a mask for oligarchical control, and we would not be satisfied, certainly not from an idealistic point of view, if in the main a few great families manipulated the political machine in their own interest. We would have to concede, of course, that states in which some of these things occurred might be democratic in form; but we would hardly be willing to describe them as democratic in fact. And certainly we could not, in our analysis of the states of the Caribbean, be content with the mere superficialities of their political forms; we would naturally wish to look below the surface and try to discover the underlying realities. Finally, perhaps, we should require of our democracy that in general there be a reasonably high standard of public morality, not a perfect standard (for uneasy thoughts might assail us of the government of some American cities) but a standard sufficiently elevated to make elections a matter of true popular choice, and not of bribery and corruption, and administration a matter of public interest, and not of private aggrandizement. All of these matters must be in the back of our minds in studying the republics under our inspection; and without some attention to each of them we should miss an essential element of our problem.

Taking all these criteria into account, the state which best meets the tests of democracy, of all the nine which we must pass in review, is Costa Rica. It happens, as we have already seen, to be one of the smallest, and it has a record of stability that is without a rival in the Caribbean.

This was not always so. In its earliest period as an independent republic, Costa Rica rivaled in turbulence and in arbitrary government the other states of Central America. Under Juan Rafael Mora, president from 1849 to 1859, and Tomás Guardia, 1870–1882, conditions were certainly more tranquil than in the previous period, but they can hardly be described as otherwise than those of dictatorship, while the years intervening between the dominance of these two strong men were years of oligarchy. The birth of democracy in Costa Rica may be said to date from the latter part of the 1880's. The election of 1889 was notable for the popular interest it aroused, for the genuine discussion of important public questions, and for the good temper with which the result was received by the defeated party. From that time to this, elections in Costa Rica have had distinctly a democratic flavor; the suffrage has been widely exercised; there has been genuine freedom of speech and of the press; there has been peaceable acceptance of the popular verdict. In the fifty-eight years that have elapsed since 1889, there has been only one *coup d'état* in Costa Rican history, the seizure of the government by Frederico A. Tinoco in 1917. Even in this case the author of the coup, though undoubtedly capitalizing on discontent with the preceding regime, which had itself shown dictatorial tendencies, did not last very long in office. Denied recognition by the neighbor states and by the United States Tinoco was compelled to relinquish power in 1919, and the course of orderly constitutional government was resumed. It seems reasonable to believe that it will not soon be broken. If Costa Rica could survive, as she did, the depression years without having recourse to the older political expedients of dictatorships and revolution, there seems reason to hope that her democratic habits have been pretty solidly formed.

Of course Costa Rican democracy does not follow precisely the pattern of the United States. For one thing,

though there are political parties, there is a much stronger
sense of allegiance to persons than to fixed principles in the
politics of this little state. In the most recent electoral contest, it is true, this was probably less the case than usual,
and the lines between conservative and liberal thought were
rather clearly drawn. But, in the main, the sense of loyalty
to individuals probably counts for more than it does in
this country. There is also a far greater centralization of
power. The president appoints the governors of the provinces, and the *jefes* or chiefs, of the subordinate cantons.
He exercises also a degree of control over the legislature
that would hardly be possible to our chief executive, except in times of emergency, or before the patronage has
been distributed at the beginning of a presidential term.
Local government is very much at the mercy of the central
administration. But none of these matters ought to be considered as altering the fundamental fact that the criteria
which we set up in this chapter are, on the whole, valid
in the case of Costa Rica. The suffrage is universal (for
males); indeed it is compulsory; elections are peaceable
(save perhaps for minor disorders); the control is not in
the hands of a few; the president is a constitutional executive; the standard of public morality, while not always
such as to satisfy the most exacting (and where would
this be true?) is on a level that excludes the worst abuses.
It is possible for Americans to be supercilious about democratic institutions in other countries; but they would have
little reason to take a gloomy view of the future of such
institutions if every country had made the progress in this
regard that Costa Rica has made in the last half century.

Next to Costa Rica among the states of the Central American galaxy, in the success with which it has operated
democratic forms, it is probably wise to put Panama. This
little republic, with less than 700,000 population, is the
youngest of all the states of Latin America, having come

into being as a result of a revolution against Colombia in 1903. In its forty odd years of history it has in general maintained excellent standards of orderly government. There was a nearly bloodless revolution in 1931, which was followed by a speedy return to constitutional forms. An amusing episode that is sometimes incorrectly described as revolution took place in 1941. The then president, Arnulfo Arias, had given many signs of partiality for the Axis, and was charged, also, with having totalitarian leanings in general. In the fall of the year, while he was on a secret visit to Havana, for reasons that had nothing to do with the public welfare, Congress declared his post vacant, and proceeded to fill it with a man of different views and of strong American sympathies. Arias was obliged to acquiesce, and remained for some time in exile. The action taken by the national legislature, while doubtless based on a technicality, was in strict conformity with the constitution, and it is therefore inaccurate to describe the events we have just recounted as "revolutionary." The fact is, I repeat, that Panama has been, on the whole, a well-conducted state, with considerable freedom of discussion, with reasonably orderly elections, and with regular acquiescence in the result of those elections. A useful, although not always a completely satisfactory test of the vitality of democratic institutions, is the number of persons who come to the polls (always assuming, of course, that the elections are really free). It is relevant to the judgment of Panama, therefore, to state that in the last national election, more than 30 per cent of the electorate participated, fully as large a number as participated in the United States. It is probably the case in Panama that a relatively small number of people play the leading role in the politics of the republic; there is, if not oligarchy, at least a tendency towards oligarchy; but, on the other hand, it is to be remembered that the landholding interests in the state are balanced by a very

considerable urban population, one-quarter of the inhabitants being concentrated in Panama and Colon.

We may turn from Panama to El Salvador. Here the
story is not quite so rosy. Between domestic revolutions,
and participation in the international wars which more
than once broke out between the Isthmian states, it is fair
to say that El Salvador's history in the nineteenth century
was a distinctly troubled one. It should be added, however,
that a great part of the difficulties of this period lay in the
fact that, owing to its geographical position, this little state
became a prey to constant interference by its neighbors.
Discontented factions in the country never hesitated to
invoke foreign aid, and by this means the country was
kept in almost continuous turmoil. By the end of the century, however, matters had begun to change for the better.
From 1898 to 1931 there was no successful revolution, and
power was transmitted from one administration to another
in an orderly manner. True, control was in the hands of
a narrow oligarchy; true, elections were pretty much dominated by the party in power; but at any rate there was
not purely personal rule; and the standards of administration, while by no means beyond criticism, were relatively
high, as compared with El Salvador's neighbors. And if, as
may well be maintained, the prelude to democracy is a
gradual improvement in the economic status of a people,
and a gradual diffusion of wealth, the prosperity that El
Salvador enjoyed in the first quarter of the twentieth century would appear to be a hopeful indication for the future.
The years of the depression, however, brought reaction in
this little state. In 1931 a president was elected who leaned
to the left, and who sponsored important reforms. The
election was hotly contested, brought out a larger vote
than usual, and was, perhaps, as nearly democratic as any
El Salvador had ever enjoyed. But the new chief executive,
Araujo, proved quite incapable of dealing effectively with

his country's problems, and a military *coup d'état* before the end of the year brought Maximiliano Martínez to the presidency, and inaugurated a dictatorship which was to last for nearly thirteen years. This strange and contradictory man, a tyrant and a theosophist, undoubtedly provided honest government, reorganized Salvadoran finances, in some measure carried on public works, and did something for education. But he was at the same time ruthless and cruel, and hardly touched—in contrast with his neighbor dictator in Guatemala—with the spirit of liberalism or of social progress. In the spring of 1944 he was compelled to put down an abortive revolt, which he did with such violence as only to aggravate and inspirit the opposition against him. In May there took place a general strike, of public officials, of school children, of various other groups. The president was compelled to resign. It is difficult to interpret what followed. In October an army man, Colonel Osman Aguirre, seized the presidency, and in January of 1945 his friend and associate, Castañeda Castro, was elected for a regular constitutional term. There is little reason to believe that the new government is inspired by any very liberal views, or that it represents new and hopeful forces in Salvadoran life. El Salvador, in the twentieth century, has not been a turbulent state; but it is certainly not yet a democracy, even by the broadest definition of terms.

Comparative tranquillity, but tranquillity under dictatorship, has been broadly characteristic of Guatemala, except in the earliest days of the period of independence. The first years of the new state were troubled, but in 1838 there appeared the first of the four great political leaders in the history of the republic, Rafael Carrera, and though not always president this man wielded the supreme power with little interruption until his death in 1865, and even transmitted it quietly to his successor. In 1871, however, began a revolution which ended in the installation in power of a second dominating personality, Justo Rufino Barrios, perhaps the most important, energetic, and constructive statesman in the annals of the republic. Barrios remained in office till 1885, when he was killed in a war he had imprudently begun for the unification of all Central America. Again, however, the presidential authority was peacefully transferred to his successor, and in 1891 an orderly and well-conducted election took place. In 1902, however, a military coup occurred which installed in the presidency another of the "strong" chief executives, Estrada Cabrera, and this amazing person retained full authority, and ruled without restraint until 1920, when popular discontent compelled his resignation. For a little the tradition of personal rule was broken and a peaceable election took place in 1926. But in 1930 came another coup which elevated Jorge Ubico to the presidency, and this statesman, the fourth of the figures of first-rate importance in Guatemalan politics, continued in office till 1944, when he was unseated by revolution. Whatever the judgment passed on many of Ubico's acts, it cannot be denied that he was a remarkable man. A soldier by profession, he rose through merit, distinguishing himself as a provincial governor by suppressing graft, taking important measures for the promotion of the public health, carrying on a vigorous campaign against yellow fever, and enforcing new standards of cleanliness upon the ignorant Indian population. In the presidency, he distinguished himself by all sorts of reforms. He built a road system which the country badly needed for the promotion of its economic life. He made an effort to abolish peonage. He improved and renovated the army. He gave great attention to the finances, enacting the so-called law of probity (by which every government official was compelled to declare his assets on entering and leaving office), balancing the budget, reducing and finally virtually extinguishing the public debt. He enacted a minimum wage law, and personally interested himself in the lot of the Indian, making an annual tour of the republic to investigate conditions in the villages. He was, it is true, completely ruthless, extremely harsh in dealing with those who opposed him, an iron-handed ruler in the strict sense of the term. But few presidents of any Central American state have a greater record of accomplishment.

Ubico was overthrown in the spring of 1944. There followed a triumvirate the dominant member of which was in the nature of a stooge for the former president. But the triumvirate was in its turn upset by revolution, and there now exists in Guatemala a government, under José Arévalo, which is apparently animated by a desire to pursue a more democratic course. How far it will be successful in doing so, and to what extent it will be forced to resort to those measures of coercion by which Guatemalan rulers usually maintain themselves in power, remains to be determined.

The history of Nicaragua is neither that of unmitigated dictatorship, of constant revolution, nor of settled order, but an interesting mixture of all three. The early history of the republic was extremely turbulent. But from 1863 to 1893, a period when the Conservative party, as it was called, was in power, there was not a single successful revolution, and power was transmitted from president to president among a small oligarchy which gave reasonably good government, and under which the country made substantial progress. In 1893 came a revolution, and the other great Nicaraguan faction, the Liberals, came into power, under José Santos Zelaya. This remarkable man accomplished some good things, especially in the field of education, but he was nonetheless a brutal and unscrupulous tyrant, who kept a good part of Central America in turmoil, as we shall have occasion to see later. His overthrow in 1909 was shortly followed by American intervention, and from 1912 to 1929 Nicaragua was, except for a brief interval, policed by American marines. Their withdrawal, after a thoroughly honest and well-conducted election, supervised by the United States, ushered in a brief period of normal constitutional government. But in 1936 came a military coup, installing in power the head of the constabulary, Anastasio Somoza, who held office until very recently and is still the real source of power. Somoza is a man of ability, though hardly a disinterested ruler. He has been interested in developing the mineral resources of the country, has extended the Pan-American highway, has enlarged (again not always disinterestedly) the country's road system, has done something for the development of hospitals, and has presided over a spectacular advance in education, the number of pupils in the schools having more than doubled since 1936. He has been in the main not so much the ruthless type of dictator as the political boss, with a keen sense of what political manipulation means. Nicaragua, in fact, could hardly be governed with the rigor which is possible in such a state as Guatemala.

This survey of Nicaraguan politics, indeed, perhaps conveys too unfavorable an impression of the possibilities of democratic progress in this colorful and interesting state. Nicaraguans have long taken a keen interest in politics, and the rivalry of the Conservative and Liberal parties, already mentioned, while often turning on personalities, and closely connected with the mutual jealousies of the two cities of Granada and León, is at least a sign of genuine political vigor. Nicaraguans, more than any other of the Central American peoples, live in towns, and it is not possible to govern an electorate of artisans, and other urban types, as it is, shall we say, the ignorant Indians of Guatemala. There is, also, more genuine discussion of political affairs in such a state than in some of its neighbors, and a broader economic base upon which to support democratic institutions. One can hardly say that today Nicaragua is a democracy; but it is possible to view the future with a tempered optimism. There has been, of recent years, a substantial advance in material prosperity; and that this advance will bring in its train more orderly conditions and more popular government certainly does not appear out of the question.

The most turbulent of all Central American states, and the last whose political history we must briefly analyze, is Honduras. It would be difficult to find, until very recently, any substantial period in which this republic was free from internecine strife; and in addition it was, until the twentieth century, again and again engaged in the international wars which constitute such a melancholy page in the history of the Isthmus. The presence of powerful foreign interests, moreover, did not always make for peace, and "banana politics" have plagued this little state in the past, along with its other difficulties. Today Honduras is ruled by a dictator, who came into power in 1931 and whose name is Tiburcio Carías. Carías is, in some ways, a relatively disinterested leader, and less ruthless than the dictators whom we have already mentioned. He has maintained himself in power longer than any of his contemporaries, and longer than any other president in the history of his country. His administration, while not remarkable for far-reaching measures of social improvement, has done something for education and for rural resettlement and agricultural reform, and something in the way of road building. In addition, his regime is said to be marked by a comparatively high standard of public administration. If not the best, it is by no means the worst in the recent history of his country or of Central America.

Let us turn now to the island republics, and first of all to Cuba. The Cubans set up their own government in 1902, when the Americans withdrew from the island. They elected one of their most highly respected personalities, Estrada Palma, as their first president, and made a good start at democratic rule. But in the elections of 1906 there were many abuses, revolution threatened, and the president, with the avowed purpose of provoking American intervention, resigned office. Once more Cuba was under tutelage, which lasted until 1909, when after the careful preparation of electoral lists, and a reasonably fair election, the troops of the United States again withdrew. While the young republic had plenty of difficulties in the next decade and a half, it was spared the most serious troubles. There was a Negro rising in 1912, but it was put down, and the elections of that year were held under relatively tranquil conditions, and were generally conceded to have been fair. In 1916, Menocal, the Conservative president elected in 1912, was chosen for a second term under conditions that pointed to widespread corruption, and which was followed by armed revolt. In 1920 and 1924 there was no marked public disorder, but, as previously, there were widespread charges of fraud. Then came Cuba's darkest period. The president elected in 1924, Gerardo Machado, was a man of competence, but he was brutal and dictatorial in method. Gradually he asserted a wider and wider measure of personal control, crushing opposition, using a strong-arm squad which stopped at no kind of terrorism to consolidate himself in power, and compelling all political parties to support him in his ambition. Such ruthless exercise of power had not been at all in the Cuban tradition in the past, and it was accepted only under duress. In course of time, the opposition to the Machadato grew; it was aided by the economic distress of the Great Depression period; it was fanned into flame in the University of Havana, and by the ABC, a group of former students and young professional men; it was given strength by the extreme measures of Machado himself; and it was finally successful in the summer of 1933 in forcing the president to relinquish power.

The story of the events of 1933 is one of great significance in the history of the republic. At first, a moderate regime came into power; but a revolution in the fall, promoted by a revolutionary junta within the army, installed a government of the Left. Never very strongly seated in the saddle, this government did not last long. It had never been able to enlist the support of the great political parties, nor was it able to command the loyalty of the army, which had undergone a revolution of its own, and had elevated to power one of the most remarkable individuals in the history of Cuba, Fulgencio Batista. There came a new overturn, then, in January 1934, and a respectable and competent regime under Colonel Mendieta entered power.

The decade (and a little more) of Cuban history since 1934 suggests on the whole a more cheerful view of the future than might be drawn from the story that we have just told. Cuba, it is true, was in no small measure dominated by the army during the first part of this period, and one president was removed from office because he could not see eye to eye with Colonel Batista on an important question of policy. But in the main this youthful soldier showed himself anything but an arbitrary tyrant, or a friend of reaction. The elections of 1936 were reasonably free from fraud. In 1939 the Cuban people elected a constitutional convention which was chosen in one of the fairest and freest elections ever held in Cuba, and in which Batista's own supporters were in a minority. This convention enacted a number of significant reforms, both in the agricultural and industrial field, and by so doing, consolidated the bases on which a healthy Cuban democracy might grow. It was followed by a presidential election in which Batista was himself a candidate; but in the electoral struggle he did not attempt to bar the field to his rivals; his success was due in great part to his great popularity, and not to the unscrupulous, illegal, and immoral methods by which more than one candidate had attained the highest office in the gift of the Cuban people. Furthermore, when in possession of power, the new executive when confronted with pressure from the military leaders, quickly put them in their places. In February of 1941, Colonel Pedraza, a leading figure in the army, and Colonel Gonzalez, a naval officer, attempted to force the president's abdication. The attempt was a stark failure; the leaders of this revolutionary plot were exiled; and constitutional government in Cuba received a significant vindication.

But something more striking was to come. Batista's term came to an end in 1944. The president declined to be a candidate for reëlection; he insisted upon the free exercise by the Cuban people of their choice of his successor; and the popular choice fell upon Dr. Grau San Martín, decidedly not one of the admirers of the previous regime. Dr. San Martín took office in the winter of 1945, and despite many difficulties he has given to Cuba since that time a government based on constitutional methods and on a rather unusual regard for administrative probity.

What, then, does this review tell us of Cuba as a democracy? On the whole, it seems fair to say that government by *coup d'état* has not been characteristic of Cuban political methods, and that the one attempt at dictatorial rule met with inglorious failure; the return to constitutionalism under Colonel Batista encourages one to believe that military domination is not congenial to Cuban opinion; the tremendous interest in politics demonstrated in almost all Cuban elections is another hopeful sign. Corruption and fraud have been plentiful in Cuban political history—plentiful to a degree perhaps unparalleled in any other state of the Caribbean; there is certainly room for a substantial improvement in Cuban public morals; but here, too, there are some encouraging signs. As to the presence of that freedom of utterance, which was one of our criteria of democratic rule, no one can doubt that Cuba qualifies, and qualifies very well indeed; indeed, the abuse of the right of speech has been commoner in the past than its suppression (except during the Machadato). All in all, then, the judgment as to the future might be one of tempered optimism; much ground remains to be won before the democratic way of life will be perfected; but this might be said of many another state besides Cuba; and it will not do for Americans, looking back upon their municipal governments of a half a century ago, for example, to be too disdainful in their judgment of the public morals of the Cuban people.

The experience of the other two island republics of the Caribbean is perhaps less hopeful. The Dominican Republic has been an independent state since it cut loose from Haiti in 1844. It was poor, weak, and distraught at the beginning; and it early fell under the control of virtual dictators, the two most important of whom were Pedro Santana and Buenaventura Baez. These men contended with one another for the mastery in the early period of independence; Santana, to consolidate his power, invited in the Spaniards in 1861; Baez was ready to do the same with the Americans a decade later. Neither one can be said to have maintained domestic order very successfully; neither one was a constructive statesman in any broad sense of the term. Baez was finally ousted from power in 1874; there ensued a period of almost continuous civil war; but in 1882 a third dictator appeared in the person of the mulatto Ulises Heureaux. Certainly not a lovable character, contemptuous of opinion as was illustrated by his famous comment that he did not care what history said of him since he would not be there to read it, ruthless, extravagant, lecherous, Heureaux at least gave the republic a period of tranquillity in which some economic progress took place. When he was assassinated in 1899, a new period of disorder followed; it was ended by the election of a strong president, Ramon Cáceres, and a brief period of constitutional rule. But once again the fatal habit of revolution assailed the Dominicans, and this led to American intervention in 1916. The marines stayed in the republic eight years; and there seemed to be better hopes of constitutional government than ever before when Horacio Vasquez assumed the presidency in 1925. The new president was a sincere and honest man, a friend to orderly process and genuine popular rule; but he fell a victim to the usual temptation of Dominican leaders to prolong their hold on power; and once again revolution took place. In 1931 General Rafael Leonidas Trujillo became chief executive; and that post he holds today, though his tenure of office was broken from 1938 to 1942. In many respects Trujillo is one of the least attractive figures that has risen to power in the Caribbean at any time. He is ruthless to a degree, and often charged by his enemies with the lavish use of the weapon of assassination. He is acquisitive beyond measure, using his public post to promote his private interests. He is inordinately vain, and has permitted such extremes of sycophancy as have rarely been tolerated even by the most absolute Latin-American rulers. He has done nothing to encourage and much to destroy the spirit of self-government among the Dominicans. He cannot evade responsibility for the hideous massacre of Haitians on Dominican soil that took place in 1937, described in an earlier chapter. At the same time it is fair to say the Trujillo regime has not been without its brighter side. The president showed great vigor in dealing with the destruction wrought by hurricane in 1931, and again in 1946. Communications, land colonization, the encouragement of rice culture, modest advances in social legislation, have characterized his rule. In no sense can that rule be called democratic; but it is possible to hope that the material progress of the country will create conditions under which democracy will function more successfully in the future than in the past, when once the dead hand of dictatorship is removed.

The last of the Caribbean states to be examined is Haiti. And here the record of the nineteenth century is certainly a very unattractive one. In the period from 1821 to 1843 a strong president, Boyer, managed to dominate affairs. But on his death there occurred the first of a series of revolutions that became a chronic feature of Haitian politics for a long time thereafter. For well over three-quarters of a century there was hardly a Haitian president who came to power by methods that even remotely smacked of popular rule, or of orderly constitutional government. Occasionally, there arose an individual who *wished* to govern by such methods, such as Salnave, or Boisrond-Canal. But the first of these two men became a dictator, and was overthrown, and the second resigned in disgust after three years of office. Moreover, far from improving, the political situation deteriorated as time went on. The years from 1883 to 1915 were Haiti's worst. Revolution succeeded revolution; the country sank deep into graft and scandal. Again and again presidents died a violent death while still in office; not one served out the term for which he was elected. A vicious circle developed; ambitious Haitian politicians managed to recruit revolutionary armies in the north, and these mercenary forces would march on Port-au-Prince and install their leader in power, only to find that a new armed force would appear, and would march on the capital in its turn. The intervention of the United States in 1915 (a matter to be treated later) brought an end to these conditions, and inaugurated a period of tranquillity in the black republic. The dozen years of Haiti's history since the American withdrawal in 1934 have also been relatively peaceful. President Vincent, who assumed power at that time, was probably less of a dictator than any chief executive in the modern history of the country. Under any circumstances, the Haitian president exercises very wide power. But Vincent was not averse to associating the legislature with him in the work of government, and he surrendered his post peaceably to his successor in 1941. In 1945, however, there again occurred a revolution in Haiti. President Lescot was overthrown, and for a brief time a military group controlled the situation. It is, however, to the credit of this group that it did not merely permit but actually encouraged a regular and constitutional election, and the present ruler of Haiti has been chosen under circumstances that give some hope of orderly and legal government.

We have now presented, in brief historical analysis, the background of the political development of the nine states that form the object of this study. Such a survey as that we have completed may, however, not do justice to the republics of the Caribbean.

In the first place, it is to be remembered that the Latin-American republics in general did not start their careers as independent states with that experience in self-government which was so striking a feature of the colonial development of Britain's American colonies. In the English-speaking colonies to the north of them the growth of representative institutions seemed to come about by an almost spontaneous process at a very early stage of their development. Virginia had a House of Burgesses as early as 1619, twelve years after the landing at Jamestown; and Massachusetts Bay, founded in 1630, was even more prompt in establishing representative assemblies. In all the colonies, indeed, the creation of a popular Assembly was soon taken for granted. No such institutions existed in the dominions of Spain. In municipal government there were the rudiments of a representative system. But, in general, the control of colonial life was in the hands of appointed authorities, and these retained a very large measure of authority up to the very end of the colonial period. The habit of discussion, of local control, of popular participation in the affairs of the colony, was not formed. True, as soon as the colonies attained their independence they quickly set up institutions in the fashion of the times, with elective legislatures intended to embody the will of the people. But the soil in which such institutions began to grow was essentially a shallow one; and from the very outset the actual control of affairs came into the hands of a few men, rather than into the hands of the mass, who were, for that matter, hardly qualified to deal with them.

In addition we must remember that the republics of the Caribbean started their careers as self-governing states on a very low level of economic development. None of them were capable of that remarkable and dynamic economic evolution which is the striking feature of American economic life in the nineteenth century. All of them had—and have— a long way to go to attain the full development of their resources. All of them lacked, in other words, the economic basis for the development of democratic institutions. It is a historical fact, to which due attention has not always been paid, that there is a connection between the wide distribution of property and the evolution of popular government. Looking at the matter from this point of view, it is not strange that it has taken time (and indeed will continue to take time) for genuine democratic government to come about in the Caribbean.

As a result of the political and economic factors which we have just considered, the tendency in the Caribbean states was towards the concentration of power in the hands of an oligarchy, at best, and in the hands of a military leader at worst. The primary condition for the development of any society is order. Order was purchased in the states of the Caribbean again and again by a too easy acceptance of the principle of personal rule. The very excesses of the Latin-American temperament, which is often impatient of control, and often swayed by strong emotional and idealistic impulses, produced their natural reaction in the sway of the *caudillo*. Constitutional forms were often perverted and distorted to serve the ambition of this or that particular leader. On paper, the political organization of the new states looked like an impressive recognition of the democratic principle. But, in actual fact, ways were found to circumvent the form of law, and to prolong and consolidate dictatorial power. Habits were set up which militated against the growth of genuine self-government, and arrested the growth of popular experience in the operation of truly popular forms. The great principle of consent, which lies at the very root of democracy, was put aside, all too often, in favor of the principle of military domination.

But to note these facts, and to understand them, is by no means to take the view that the situation in the Caribbean republics is an unchanging one, or that there is no hope of the further development of democratic institutions. In the first place (and this is of cardinal importance), there can be little doubt of the strength of the movement of democratic aspiration in most of these states. A wise and experienced commentator on Latin-American affairs put the matter in a nutshell when he stated, "If the Latin-American states are not democracies, they want to be." The truth of this observation is attested by the steady loyalty which all these states have shown, in theory, to the constitutional forms associated with genuine popular rule. Read, one after the other, the fundamental law of the republics of the Caribbean, and you could form no other conviction than that these communities were committed to the democratic principle. And the same point may be illustrated by an instructive incident which happened to a traveler to Guatemala only a few years ago. He was carrying into the country Chester Lloyd Jones's excellent study on the region, a chapter of which is headed, "If I Were Dictator." His book was confiscated by the customs authorities because it suggested that Guatemala was not a constitutional republic. President Ubico, though he wielded immense power, always referred to himself as "constitutional President," and he was, one sees, extremely sensitive to any charge of absolutism. The matter may appear to be merely trivial, but it is not. If hypocrisy is the tribute that vice pays to virtue, then deference to constitutional form is the tribute paid to democracy by those who, while violating its principles, admit its fundamental validity, and its basic appeal to the instincts of those they serve.

The existence of this democratic idealism is not the only hopeful factor in the situation, so far as the future is concerned. By any fair and reasonable test, the tendency of Caribbean government has been, on the whole, and with some reservations, along progressive rather than regressive lines. If, for example, we ask ourselves whether or not there has been an advance in respect for public order in the Caribbean there can be but one answer. The continuous civil wars that were so striking a feature of Central American politics in the nineteenth century, and in the first decade of the twentieth, have disappeared. Panama, as we have seen, has been on the whole a tranquil state during its forty-odd years of independent life. Cuba, if we look at its history from 1902 to 1946, has a better record by far than any one of the Continental republics in the first forty years of its history, in the period from the eighteen twenties to the eighteen sixties. There has been at least comparative tranquillity in Haiti and the Dominican Republic in the last decade and a half.

Of course tranquillity is not democracy. But even such a repulsive tyranny as that of Trujillo in the Dominican Republic is better than constant civil war, and a more favorable breeding ground for that economic and social progress on which democratic government depends.

What is more, we must not assume that it is only in tranquillity that an advance has been made. Civilian, as distinguished from military, government is making headway in the Caribbean. Today in Costa Rica, in Panama, in Guatemala, in Cuba, and in Haiti the chief office of state is in civilian hands. While too much ought not to be made of these facts, they are worth noting. And, to state the matter conversely, it can be said with some assurance that today there is in no one of the republics, with the exception of the Dominican Republic, a brutal and ruthless despotism of the type that has all too often been associated with some of them in the past.

In addition to all this, it seems fair to say that for many of these states there lies ahead a hope for an economic development that will contribute to political stability, and to the establishment of a more democratic regime. We cannot be, in this respect, too optimistic about Haiti. But the Dominican Republic certainly has real possibilities, Cuba is a land of very great natural resources, and most of the Central American republics present an opportunity for substantial economic advancement. It is possible to assume that with the growth of a material prosperity, and with the wider diffusion of economic well-being, the way will be paved for an improvement in the political institutions of these various communities. We cannot, of course, make confident prophecy about a future which has still to be unfolded; but we shall not be sanguine beyond the bounds of reason if we assume that the possibility of progress exists. We must not expect, of course, in any case, the attainment in a brief period of our political maturity; but some improvement in the essentials, a decline in the influence of the military, a greater respect for constitutional forms, a progressive improvement in the quality of the electorate through more prosperous conditions of life, and their concomitants, the spread of education, and the development of a larger middle class, which desires peace and order—all these are such changes as can conceivably come about in the future. Whether they *do* come about depends upon many factors, and not the least of these is the attitude of the United States towards its neighbors, and the success which we here in America may meet with in making our own political system function for the benefit of all, and without serious dislocation. But in so far as this phase of the matter is concerned, we may well postpone discussion until we come to examine in detail the relations of the Caribbean states with their great northern neighbor.

But what, it will be asked, of the rival philosophies that exist in the world today? Is there not a genuine danger that our southern neighbors will fall a victim to the blandishments of the apostles of totalitarianism? Is there not danger of some such neo-Fascist experiment in one or another of the Caribbean states as Colonel Perón appears to be instituting in Argentina? Or, contrariwise, is there not danger of Communism? Here is an interesting and, indeed, an important question, and one that needs to be examined in some detail.

Before we answer a question of this kind, we must take care to be more precise in our thinking with regard to these matters than many Americans are. The words Fascist and Communist have become packed with emotional content during the last decade; they often constitute an appeal to intense feeling and bitter prejudice rather than an attempt to describe accurately the position of those to whom they are applied. Unless we have such an idea, it is really quite useless to discuss the question as to whether we are in danger of one or the other.

Nor is it reasonable to assume, as is sometimes done, that the contrast to be made between democracy and totalitarianism is defined by the existence of a system of free enterprise on the one hand and of state control on the other. Every civilized state puts some restrictions on the economic liberty of the citizen, and even in the United States the number of these restrictions generally accepted, that are no longer the subject of partisan debate or personal resentment, is greater than it has ever been in our history. No intelligent person would describe post-war Britain as either Fascist or Communist, but that the liberty of the citizen has there been restricted to a wholly unprecedented degree is beyond doubt. If we are to talk of totalitarianism intelligently, we had best begin by defining it carefully, and with scrupulous regard for the real meaning of words. Let us see with what success we can tackle this problem.

The first sign manual of the totalitarian state, it seems to me, is that the totalitarian does not accept dictatorship as an expedient for dealing with a special situation, as did the Romans in ancient times, to take one example; he regards it as a fundamental principle from which his whole system of government flows. The Fuehrerprinzip, to use the German term, is of the very essence of the totalitarian idea. The leader is all-powerful; from him the authority of the state is derived; and from him it must be transmitted to a successor that is no less powerful than he. No restriction of legal form applies to him, at least in theory; he embodies the state; he operates in a realm which is beyond criticism and beyond control. This concentration of power in the individual, as the basis of all political organization, is fundamental.

Behind the individual stands the party, the monolithic political machine. It is through this instrument that the dictatorship works; and within its ranks are those who are politically influential, and whose loyalty to the totalitarian ideal has been thoroughly proved. On its higher levels there may be a measure of discussion; but the rank and file are rather the executants than the determinants of the policy of the state. They are in some degree privileged; but they must, of course, pay allegiance to the totalitarian theory, and must not deviate from the line that is laid down by those at the top of the party pyramid.

A second conception that seems basic from the angle of

totalitarian theory is that the educational system of the state is devised to fortify the point of view that has just been described. In the schools the young must, from the beginning, be indoctrinated with the conception of obedience to the authority of the state; the teaching of any doctrine, the presentation of any material which runs counter to the accepted tenets of the totalitarian creed must be totally excluded; the whole apparatus of public opinion, indeed, must be directed by those who accept the totalitarian doctrine; dissent must be rigidly excluded; and the people must, from the cradle to the grave, be fed predigested opinions, and their ideas of both their own and the outside world formed by a rigorous process of control. It is not enough (and here is a point that needs to be emphasized) that censorship should exclude ideas that may run counter to the policies of the public authorities; there must be a resolute and consistent effort through the educational system, through the press, and through the radio, to form the public mind positively. And behind the effort to do this there stands, as an essential feature of state organization, a secret police which roots out dissent, and which punishes by appropriate measures those who dare to differ with the regime.

A third essential element in a truly totalitarian system is the complete control of the economic life of the state. The very word "totalitarian" implies this. It is not only in their political opinions that the people of a Fascist state are controlled. On the contrary, their whole economic life is subject to rigorous supervision. The mechanism of international trade is brought completely under state supervision. The problems of domestic finance are solved by public authority. The conditions of industrial life, the determination of appropriate forms of economic activity, are fixed by those who control the mechanism of the state, not by those engaged in the actual processes of production. Labor unions, if they exist at all, are under the strictest and most rigorous domination, and the right to strike does not exist. Immigration and emigration are regulated according to the interests of the regime. The most far-reaching interference in the life of the individual, from the viewpoint of his economic activities, is taken for granted.

Finally, as an essential element (in the totalitarianism of the Right, at least), we may note the existence of a furious nationalism, and of a tendency towards militarism. The Fascist states which have just gone down to ruin in World War II were states in which aggression was unblushingly preached, and as unblushingly practiced. The piling up of armaments, the public avowal of the doctrine that the world belongs to the strong, the cynical attitude assumed towards any effort to introduce a little order and reason and good will into the intercourse of nations, these are striking features of the doctrines of a Hitler or a Mussolini. They are, indeed, the thing that made totalitarian dictatorships of the Right extremely dangerous, and plunged the whole world into strife. They represent the culmination of the totalitarian idea, and make the organization of the life of the state center on conquest and international strife.

When all the characteristics which we have just mentioned are united, when there is an institutionalized dictatorship, complete control of opinion, total domination of the economy of the state, and a furious and aggressive nationalism, we can talk accurately of totalitarianism. It is possible that we might use the term with a fair measure of justice if the first three of these four characteristics were present. But certainly we must not talk as if the mere existence of dictatorship was in itself a proof of these noxious doctrines; certainly we must not confuse the historical forms of personal control that have marked the development of many Latin-American states with the systematic acceptance of the totalitarian idea. When we use our terms carefully, indeed, and do not fall a victim to that kind of loose writing and loose talking that creates so many perils for us in every field, we shall be in a better position to judge the future prospects of anti-democratic movements in the Caribbean.

Let us look first, for example, at this question of institutionalized dictatorship. The dictatorships of the Caribbean area have been anything but institutionalized. In fact, it is very much in the pattern of Latin-American politics for one state or another to react against a dictator, and it is almost invariably the case that a dictator finds great difficulty in passing on his authority to a successor of his own choice. At the present moment, dictatorship even of the limited kind that has often existed in the Caribbean is to be found, strictly speaking, only in one state, Honduras, and in one of the island states, the Dominican Republic.

What is fully as important, almost always, in the countries we are studying, is that dictatorship is masked in constitutional forms. This we have already seen to be the case, as in President Ubico's dislike of the term dictator to describe his own position in the state.

The same point may be illustrated by the fact that no Caribbean dictator in any modern period, at any rate, has had the temerity to suggest for himself a life term. He may be quite willing to tinker with the Constitution to prolong his tenure of office, and he may often get away with such an expedient. But for him to assume, as Hitler and Mussolini assumed, that his authority was coterminous with his own life, would be a virtual impossibility. And in actual practice it would be difficult to find an instance (with the exception of Carrera in Guatemala) in which the ruler of any one of the states which we have been analyzing had managed to hang on to power until death terminated his career. It is not in the temper of the peoples of the Caribbean area to take kindly to any such concentration of authority; such a concentration is not to be found in their history; and it is, probably, less likely today than it has ever been.

When it comes to the control of the agencies of opinion,

it is easily seen that no such ambitious system of regimentation is possible in the region we are examining, speaking
generally, as is possible in the Fascist states of the Old World.
Nowhere in any of the countries which we are studying is
there a *cult* of dictatorship, that is, systematic instruction in
a totalitarian ideology. As a matter of fact, the educational
systems of most of the Caribbean republics are not sufficiently highly developed to make such a thing possible. But
within the limits of the actual there is no attempt, and has
not been any attempt, on the part of any political leader, to
indoctrinate with the totalitarian point of view. In the
Dominican Republic at the present time there is a disgust-
ing amount of servile praise of the dictator in the public
schools; but this is a very different thing from the exaltation
of a system, and it would be fairer to say that President
Trujillo, by his extension of a system of public instruction,
is preparing the way for the downfall of the kind of regime
he represents than to regard him as the founder of the Fascist state, or as the embodiment of the Fuehrer principle.
It may be doubted, indeed, whether the people of the Caribbean area are much interested in any systematic ideology,
or if they have reached that stage of cultural development
where such an ideology could take root widely or receive
a very generous acceptance. Authoritarianism they understand, but it is, as we have seen, the authoritarianism of the
individual leader, not of the leader as the embodiment of
a system.

Still more unlikely, it may well be argued, is the development in the regions we are discussing of the total control
of the economy by the state. The possibility of such control
depends in no very small degree upon the national temperament. Germans, for example, seem to be endowed with a
rather extraordinary degree of docility. Russians are habitu-
ated to rather drastic regimentation. But not all peoples react
in the same way to regulation. The Latin-American tem-

perament, if one may generalize about it perhaps a little too broadly, does not seem to accept at all readily the direction of the state, especially in economic affairs. And it so happens that we have had, in the course of the last few years, a very interesting illustration of the relative willingness of the people of many nations to submit to measures of social control. From the theoretical point of view, during the recent war, the case for drastic price control, and for the prevention of inflation, was tolerably clear, so clear that even our own highly individualistic people accepted it as a necessity. But in most of the states which we have been studying, as has been seen, there was not very effective price control, even by the American standard; in most of them there has been a very substantial rise in prices; in most the motive of private gain has proven stronger than the possibilities of public action. What has been true under the conditions of war is still more likely to be true under the conditions of peace, and ought to make it fairly clear that the substitution of a state-directed for a relatively free economy would be a difficult matter in the republics of the Caribbean. Of course, in saying this, it is not to be assumed that in this part of the world, as elsewhere, there will not be in the future more state intervention rather than less; this is the tendency of the times; it is as true of democratic states as of absolute ones; but the test lies not in this individual instance or that of the extension of public authority, but rather in the willing acceptance of such extension, and in the attempt to carry such extension to its extreme limit. Nothing in the experience of the last few years suggests that any such attempt is imminent with any one of our southern neighbors.

As for the possibilities of aggressive militarism or anything of that kind, if it should appear at all in the future it does not seem at all likely that it will be linked with totalitarian philosophy. There have been trouble-makers in the Caribbean, as elsewhere. The efforts of the ridiculous Soulouque to reconquer the Dominican Republic are reduced to comedy by their very inefficiency, but an abler man might conceivably have accomplished much harm. The career of Barrios in Guatemala, and his attempt by armed force to create, or rather to re-create, a Central American Union, was more dangerous. Zelaya in Nicaragua was a constant trouble-maker until his overthrow in 1909. But it is significant that no one of the Caribbean dictators of the more recent period has been militantly nationalist and jingo; and there has not been an international war in Central America for the last thirty years. Central American presidents, like other politicians, do, from time to time, attempt to buttress their personal popularity by nationalistic gestures, by defying somebody or something outside their borders; but there has been little evidence in the last quarter of a century of that furious nationalism that is one of the principal vices and one of the principal dangers of our times. After all, when one comes down to the nub of the matter, no one of the republics we are considering is strong enough to cut much of a figure in international conflict; war is an extremely expensive luxury, and preparation for war on an extensive scale hardly less so; and the peril of starting something that one cannot finish, or of inviting outside interference, must be a real one to any Caribbean politician.

Arguing thus, from the angle of pure theory, or even on the basis of past experience, there seem many reasons why the establishment of totalitarian forms in the Caribbean would seem to be a difficult matter. But this does not mean that we ought to assume that Fascist and Communist influences may not, from time to time, prove embarrassing in our relations with our neighbors. The dictatorships of the Right, it is true, have been temporarily discredited by the grisly fate of Hitler and of Mussolini. Even the less "total" regimes of Franco in Spain and of Salazar in Portugal do not appear to have aroused any very intense admiration in any part of the Caribbean area. But if Colonel Perón succeeds in introducing his neo-Fascist ideas into the Argentine (and at the present writing it looks as if he might, at least for a time), we might conceivably see some of that spirit reflected in other parts of Latin America. In particular, the intense nationalism that is connected with the Argentine creed might communicate itself to other states, and affect their policies adversely so far as outside interests were concerned. This might not be Fascism in the literal sense of the term, but it would be an infection not unconnected with the Fascist spirit, and one that would certainly tend to check the healthy development of the democratic idea.

In the same way, it is impossible to deny that there are various practices all too readily adopted by Latin-American dictators that, while not Fascist, have a kind of Fascist flavor. In the Dominican Republic, for example, there is something very like one-party rule, though occasionally President Trujillo permits other political groups to take a hand in affairs as a kind of window dressing. Something of the same situation has existed in Honduras under Carías. In more than one state, interference with the freedom of the press has been and is practiced. The opponents of the regime may be subjected to restraints, or even to downright persecution. All these things are, of course, disquieting to the believer in popular rule.

On the other hand, such deviations must not be taken too seriously. They look away from the democratic ideal, but they do not suggest, in any well-balanced and mature judgment, that totalitarianism is just around the corner. They are, on the whole, to be taken as a part of the context of Caribbean life, as it has developed historically, rather than the sinister omens of a new political system similar to those that have just been put down in Europe. There is no genuine reason to be unduly apprehensive with regard to the growth of neo-Fascism in the region we are discussing.

But if not Fascism, what of Communism? Must we view

such a movement with more apprehension? Will totalitarian
ideas come to the Caribbean, not from the Right but from
the Left, and will they take root there? This is an interesting question, and one that deserves a careful examination.
One might begin by arguing, of course, that the same considerations that make Fascism unlikely militate also against
Communism. The Latin-American temperament, as we have
seen, is not well adapted to any totalitarian conception. And,
in addition to this, other facts must be added. On the whole,
Communism may be described as an industrial faith. On
the whole, it has made very little headway among peasant
populations, and it is significant that in Eastern Europe,
where regimes of the Left have installed themselves in power
since the war, they have moved very cautiously in dealing
with the farmers, and have made little effort towards the
collectivization of agriculture, which was carried through
at such terrible cost in Russia itself. The states of the Caribbean are, it has already been noted, for the most part, agricultural economies. The rural population might, of course,
at a given moment become discontented, and at such a
moment it might make common cause with other elements
in a movement of the Left; but it would, in all probability,
be difficult to persuade it to accept a genuine totalitarianism. It would be more attracted by a program of land redis-
tribution than by a collectivization of agriculture, or by
sweeping measures of state control in general.

There are important elements in every Latin-American
state that would oppose the growth of Communism. It goes
without saying that the upper and middle classes would do
so. So far as past experience indicates anything, it seems to
show that the military power in the Caribbean is not very
likely to fall into the hands of the Leftists. Army groups,
indeed, are rather likely to be found on the conservative side.
The leaders of dictatorial temper, wherever they rise to
power, are not likely to be infected with radical ideas, but

are more probably instruments of reaction. They are, in the nature of the case, not interested in theories—and besides, the greater number of them have signalized their elevation to office by determined efforts to woo the United States, while of course flirting and coquetting, as occasion offers, with those whom we dislike. That a free election would bring about a Communist regime in any Caribbean state is, at this writing, exceedingly improbable; that revolution would accomplish the same result is within the bounds of possibility, but hardly to be reckoned an immediate danger.

There is, also, one other factor that must be considered in assessing the forces of resistance to Communism. The power of the Catholic Church, as we shall see, varies immensely in the different republics of the Caribbean. But wherever it is an influence at all, it is, of course, the resolute enemy of Communism. No general view of the situation that omits consideration of this fact could possibly be regarded as a complete one.

But plausible as is this argument that Communism can hardly take root in the Caribbean, we must not carry that argument too far. It is, here as elsewhere, in a stronger position than Fascism. The latter is a discredited system, and a discredited word. Communism is a going concern in one of the greatest countries of the world, and it makes a positive appeal, an appeal far more positive than its rival, to the intense yearning for improving the condition of the masses that is characteristic of our age. It has a dynamism of its own; and the existence of Communist parties within the democratic fabric of the states of Europe provides a constant basis for effective propaganda, and for the promotion of its cause. The Communists, indeed, by accepting the democratic processes of the West, can use their situation to promote their doctrines, and lay the foundations of a revolutionary movement by the appropriate tactical measures, either of reform or of obstruction and agitation. They have, of course, at bottom, no respect for the democratic way. Let them secure possession of the key posts in the civil administration, or, still more, in the military, and they might conceivably find a way to set up a regime of their own. That they could long maintain themselves in power may be doubtful. That they could carry through a sweeping and thorough program of Communization may also be doubtful. But it would be misleading to deny that the existence of a totalitarian ideology of the Left is a factor to be considered in connection with the Caribbean republics. Nor is it to be gainsaid that further industrial developments are likely to add to the strength of such a movement, and to give it a greater part in the future than it has played in the past.

At present, it is true, in many states Communism is a very feeble thing indeed. In most of the states of Central America, Communist parties can hardly be said to exist. The one exception to this generalization is Costa Rica. There a political group so labeled was formed in 1930. Its leader, Manuel Mora, is a prominent and widely respected individual. Its program, so far as specifics are concerned, has not been a very radical or far-reaching one. Even its name has been changed with time, and this group now calls itself the Vanguardia Popular. It polled about 17 per cent of the votes in 1942, and has had a few representatives in Congress. There seems little reason to disbelieve that it has some kind of connection with Moscow. But as an immediate peril to the tranquillity of the state it does not look very impressive. Communist influence has certainly penetrated some of the Costa Rican trade unions, has been reflected in the development of a Farmer's Union, and has expressed itself in a youth movement. But, up to the present time, it has not brought about any serious social unrest, and has conformed to the democratic method, at least on the surface. It is, of course, impossible to prophecy what its future trend will be.

In the island states, a weak Communist movement has recently emerged in Haiti, and an even weaker one in the Dominican Republic. But the situation is far otherwise in Cuba. There the movement of the Left is stronger than in any other of the Caribbean states, and has had a longer history. The Communist party was organized in the republic as early as 1925, but in the first years its growth was slow, largely confined to foreigners, and its members were recruited in the light industries rather than in the fundamental sectors of Cuban economic life. But with the coming of the Great Depression the situation changed, and an effort was made to extend the party's organization, and to broaden its activities. There is no doubt that some success was attained, but politically the results were not impressive. In the presidential elections of the last decade, the Communists have not appeared in the field under their own name. But in the elections of 1944 the Partido Social Democrático, which has been described as "frankly Communist," polled 122,000 votes, and elected a considerable number of the members of the legislature. Indeed, President Grau San Martín has secured majority support for his government by a four-party alliance in which the group just mentioned is represented.

In the Cuban trade unions this same Left wing group is strongly representative. The Confederation of Cuban Workers, as constituted today, is a powerful factor in the politics of the island. Its executive committee is about evenly balanced between the representatives of the president's party, known as the Auténticos, and the representatives of the Partido Social. Its avowed and recognized leader belongs to the latter group, and is said to maintain a very high degree of control over the organization itself.

There is always danger in attempting to be precise about the extent of Communist influence in any political or economic unit. In every country it is easy to affix the Communist label to any individual or association of individuals that is to the Left of one's own views. The really crucial question, the question as to whether a given individual or group reject the democratic method, and are, at heart, frankly in favor of the totalitarian ideal, and of revolutionary methods of attaining it, is one that it is particularly difficult to answer. Probably many members of the so-called Communist groups in the Caribbean would not themselves have a clear-cut answer to this question, but are merely profoundly discontented and disillusioned with the existing economic order. We do not need to become unduly apprehensive about the future if only the way is found to deal constructively with current economic and political problems. It ought to be almost axiomatic that the answer to the totalitarian menace —if menace there be in any given case—lies not in mere repression, but in positive measures of economic and social amelioration.

It is here, of course, that the question of the future of democracy in the Caribbean inevitably relates to the policy of the United States. For the prosperity and the progress of these republics is in no small degree dependent upon American policy and upon the American example. Our influence in this region is very great; our economic connection with it extremely close. To the cool observer, it would seem as if only a series of incredible blunders could alienate these states from a country with which they have such close relations, or make possible the establishment of a regime in any one of them that was frankly based upon a widely differing economic and political system. But with these observations, we enter the field of American policy and of foreign affairs; and further comment on this side of the matter we shall accordingly postpone till a later chapter of this volume.

4. The Social Structure

We have now analyzed the political and economic conditions which exist in the states of the Caribbean. It is necessary to turn to the social life of these republics before we discuss their relations with the United States. And it is, of course, impossible to do this without candidly stating at the outset that there exists in all these countries (as, indeed, elsewhere) a vast amount of remediable misery, and that the improvement of their status is a matter of concern, not only to themselves, but to us as well. Much may be done, as we shall see, through the processes of inter-American coöperation; but not everything can so be done; much depends, of course, upon the people themselves, and especially upon men of social vision and administrative energy in the various countries we have been examining.

The fundamental weakness of many of these states, from the angle of social improvement, is the absence of a substantial middle class. In all of them, there exists an upper class, often well educated, cultured in many respects, and quite able to give a good account of itself from the point of view of native intelligence and capacity. In all of them there exists a depressed majority, which is existing on a standard of living that would seem positively pitiable to most Americans. What is largely lacking is a social stratum which is neither rich nor poor; which, having itself risen, is on the whole favorably disposed to seeing others rise, which has no preference for oligarchy, because it does not provide the oligarchs, which values education and kindred forms of social amelioration because it can take advantage of them, and which wishes good order and democratic rule because it will gain from both. Of course, such a generalization must be taken *cum grano*, and there are obvious exceptions to the general rule. In Costa Rica, as we have already seen, the free farmers form the mass of the population, and provide just the outlook that we are talking about. In Cuba the immense wealth of the country has given rise to a substantial middle class which is a healthy force in politics. And there are obviously shopkeepers, artisans, and the like in the cities of every one of the republics, and independent farmers in the rural districts. But in the main the above statement holds; a sufficiently large middle group does not exist in most of the societies that we have been examining.

Such a situation might be remedied if the governing class, in any case small, were fired by an ardent desire to improve the situation of the masses. That this is not always the case is not a matter of too great reproach to the citizens of the Caribbean republics; for selfishness among the well-to-do and the fortunate is certainly not an exclusively Caribbean phenomenon. Yet in some cases the indifference of the elite to the welfare of the great majority is striking. In Haiti, for example, the small governing clique is, on the whole, pitifully indifferent to the condition of the peasantry, and yet it is only from this class that there can be recruited the persons who would by their persistent efforts improve the situation. What is true of Haiti is true in lesser degree of the ruling groups in some other of the countries we have been examining; they are often pretty much concerned with the maintenance of the *status quo*. They would not think of themselves, of course, in quite this light; but the sacrifices that would be required of them to provide for a substantial improvement in the condition of the masses would undoubtedly be resisted in many cases. In many cases, but not by any means in all. The Caribbean is like other parts of the world; the spirit of social amelioration which is a part of our age has touched it as it has touched virtually every civilized society; but the satisfaction of that spirit is a slow and laborious matter.

It might be thought that some impetus to the work of social progress would be brought about by the growth of a labor movement. Most historians, I fancy, would be of the opinion that in the long run the aspirations of labor have corresponded with the improvement of social conditions in general. But, unhappily, the labor movement is still in its infancy in many of the states which we have been examining. The great exception is Cuba, where there is a very strong movement, and one, as we have seen, that is over-saturated with Communist influences. There has been a substantial development of the labor movement in Costa Rica in the last decade, and the right to organize and the right to strike were formally recognized by the Labor Code adopted in 1942. The recent revolution in Guatemala was in part brought about by the activities of the trade unions. But in such a state as Haiti there is no labor movement at all; President Trujillo has not permitted any to exist in the Dominican Republic; President Carías has frowned upon any such nonsense as trade unions in Honduras. Such ameliorative tendencies, then, as stem from the existence of a lively and aggressive working class, are not likely to be found in some of the Caribbean republics. And only in the two that we have mentioned is there any reason to look forward to the influence of labor in politics as a force of substantial significance.

There is another difficulty in the way of social progress in the states of the Caribbean. These countries, by the comparative standard, are most of them poor; their national incomes and their national budgets alike are small; the funds for ambitious social programs have not yet been found. This is a point that deserves amplification, but before enlarging upon it it is necessary to say that Latin-American statistics often leave something to be desired. The observations to be made must be taken, not as absolute, but as suggestive and relative; the figures given are approximations, nothing more. With this word of warning, let us note, first of all, the estimated national incomes of the countries we are studying, as given in a volume published by the Coordinator of Inter-American Affairs in 1944.

	Total (*in thousands of dollars*)	*Per capita* (*in dollars*)
Costa Rica	94,680	134
Cuba	551,000	115
Guatemala	303,660	88
Nicaragua	62,870	61
Honduras	68,040	58
El Salvador	103,000	55
Panama	45,000	71
Dominican Republic	100,460	51
Haiti	54,390	20

These figures (even when allowance is made for a scale of monetary values very different from our own) give one some idea of the difficulties in the way of far-reaching programs of social improvement; but it is possible to put the matter still more strikingly. The expenditures of the various governments under their annual budgets are, of course, by no means all of them spent for the amelioration of present conditions; much naturally goes to the army and the administrative machine. But the per capita expenditure of these governments is at least an imperfect measure of the possibilities of the moment. These per capita expenditures, (and again we must emphasize the purely approximate character of such calculations) were as follows for the budgetary year 1942–43, if not otherwise stated: Cuba, $23.62; Costa Rica, $14.35; Panama, $33.81; Nicaragua, $9.00; Dominican Republic, $7.26; El Salvador, $5.07; Honduras, $4.60; Guatemala, $4.20; Haiti, $2.22. To make these figures more meaningful, it is sufficient to remark that the city of Chicago expends on its municipal services about $90.00 per capita a year, and this is exclusive of state and federal services.

With such slender resources, and with such a limited national income on which to draw, and with what is possibly a less acutely felt need of reform than exists in such a country as the United States, it is easy to see why the states of the Caribbean are in many respects less advanced than their well-wishers would desire. They also face, and must face for some time, conditions that are far from satisfactory in the field of public health, and in the field of education; and though there is little doubt that the tendency is upward, rather than downward, there is an immense amount of ground to be won.

The importance of education in the life of any progressive community can hardly be overstressed. It is not formal instruction alone that is important; it is the opportunity for self-improvement, and the desire for self-improvement that is stimulated by the process of instruction, that is the most significant thing about any educational program. Yet education, in many of the Caribbean republics, is in far from a satisfactory state, and the problems connected with its improvement are enormous. The worst case, no doubt, is that of Haiti. The obstacles in the way of an ambitious program in this community are tremendous. The masses themselves are apathetic; the elite fear the social consequences that may follow on any great spread of enlightenment. The language of the cultivated class is French; the language of the peasantry is Creole; and the teacher, who is struggling upwards himself in the social scale, is likely to prefer to speak the language that gives him social distinction rather than the one which is most intelligible to his hearers. The recruiting of the teaching class has been extremely difficult, especially in view of the low salaries paid (about $13 a month at the present time); the standard of the teachers themselves has been extremely low, many of them indeed being hardly able to teach the 3 R's; the instruction itself is likely to be unrelated to the needs of those for whom it exists. The Americans in their occupation of Haiti attempted to set up agricultural schools, whose programs of instruction should be tied in with Haiti's major industry, and whose students would go out to instruct the peasants; the idea behind this experiment was an excellent one; but the political opposition on the part of the Haitian intelligentsia was extreme. It would not be fair to say that there is a hopeless situation; more and more people are undoubtedly aware of the importance of the problem; but the practical difficulties in the way of carrying out a full-fledged program are immense.

Haiti, of course, represents an extreme; at the other pole with regard to education is the little state of Costa Rica. Costa Ricans are deservedly proud of their achievements in this field, and this very pride ensures that the progress that they have already made will be continued. No small part of their achievement is due to a great personality, Mauro Fernandez, who was the country's educational pioneer, and who secured the enactment of a law for free, compulsory secular education as far back as 1886. On the basis of this fundamental statute there has been developed a school system which gives at least the elements of education to every Costa Rican child, which provides for higher education in the principal towns, and which conducts to the state university those most ambitious and fortunate. Salaries in the Costa Rican schools are low; there is some political influence (often complained of by the teachers themselves);

and it is certainly not possible to compare the Costa Rican educational organization with that of the most advanced and opulent of modern states; but considering the resources on which the country has to draw, the results are impressive, and offer a splendid example to the rest of Central America.

Cuba, like Costa Rica, is in the vanguard of the Caribbean states in the field of education. It has made substantial progress during recent years; the use of the army for purposes of instruction, under the Batista regime, however it might be criticized from one point of view, certainly produced results; and the crown of the Cuban educational system, the University of Havana, has on its faculty men who, in distinction and scholarship, may well be compared with those of any other land.

It would be superfluous in this brief study to analyze the various republics one by one. It is fair to say that the educational leaven is working in most of them; that even such a dictator as Trujillo, for example, despite the gross selfishness of his regime in many respects, has shown much interest in the schools of his country, and that the war and the encouragement of the United States have, as we shall see later, stimulated no small measure of educational progress. Yet the fact remains that the situation in many of these states is far from satisfactory. A rough test as to the matter may be made through the statistics of literacy; and we may be pretty sure that these statistics do not exaggerate the extent of ignorance in any of the countries concerned. Here are the facts in this regard. Costa Rica, 82 per cent; Cuba, 60 per cent; Panama, 65 per cent; Honduras, 52 per cent; Guatemala, 33 per cent; the Dominican Republic, 33 per cent; Nicaragua, 30 per cent; El Salvador, 21 per cent; Haiti, 8 per cent. Another measure of the state of the public mind is to be found in the circulation of newspapers, and here, too, with the necessary reserves, it is worth while to state the matter in figures, relating them to the population of the country. In Panama probably one person in ten reads a newspaper; in Cuba 1 in 18; in Costa Rica 1 in 35; in El Salvador 1 in 48; in Honduras 1 in 50; in the Dominican Republic 1 in 74; in Nicaragua 1 in 120; in Guatemala 1 in 138; in Haiti 1 in 544. These figures, of course, express a current situation; and they do not measure, or even suggest, the interest in educational progress which exists in most of the Caribbean states. But they do, of course, make clear that there is much to be done before the conditions for intellectual progress are entirely satisfactory.

If the situation with regard to education is not all that it ought to be in the states of the Caribbean, the same thing may be said with regard to public health. Here, indeed, is a problem of the greatest urgency and insistency. For in tropical lands the greatest enemy to progress is not the climate, taken by and of itself; the enemy is the depleting, yet not usually fatal, diseases which are characteristic of such lands, and which interpose a constant barrier to economic and social progress. Perhaps the most dreadful of these diseases is malaria, which, in the words of a Guatemalan health authority, "decimates the population, reduces the activity and energy of the workers, depresses the intelligence of the children, and diminishes fecundity." In such a country as the United States, Americans are apt to think of this malady as mildly intermittent; in many of the states below the Rio Grande it has a chronic character. It *does* kill, and on an important scale; but fully as serious is its effect upon those who suffer from it and continue to live. To discover it, to deal with it effectively, and in course of time to reduce its ravages, is a tremendous task, and one for which, as we have seen, the resources of the Caribbean states are in many cases far from sufficient. Another disease, dramatized in the United States by the work of the Rockefeller Institute and by the disinterested labors of

C. W. Styles after the Spanish-American War, is hookworm. The hookworm parasite enters the body through the soles of the feet, and results in a kind of tropical anemia which is very debilitating. According to a study made by the International Labor Office, the productive capacity of a worker suffering from this disease is reduced by about 50 per cent. The remedy for hookworm is clear; since the parasite is discharged in the feces, reasonably good sanitary arrangements, and the wearing of shoes, will sharply reduce the incidence of the malady; but both the one and the other of these things depend upon an increase in public interest and in public well-being. There is, here again, a great problem, and a central one.

The care and treatment of disease in general may occupy us for a moment in this attempt to portray briefly the social conditions in the states of the Caribbean. Conditions are distinctly good in one of the republics we have been examining; in Cuba, for example, there has been for some time a very active interest in medicine. The path to the discovery of yellow fever was illuminated by a great Cuban scholar, Carlos Finlay; and the present president of the republic is a medical man of distinction. In Cuba there is one doctor to every 1313 people; and while this proportion is not, of course, as great as that in the United States, it is impressively large by a less exacting standard. But there is no other of the Caribbean states in anything like as good a case as the Pearl of the Antilles; the proportions for the other republics are as follows: Panama, 1 in 3270; Costa Rica, 1 in 3759; Nicaragua, 1 in 4723; Dominican Republic, 1 in 4759; Guatemala, 1 in 6568; Honduras, 1 in 7985; El Salvador, 1 in 8722; Haiti, 1 in 11,904. These figures are, in no case, impressive; but they would probably look even less favorable than they do if account were taken of the tendency of the medical profession to concentrate in the towns. There are parts of the Caribbean area, indeed, such as rural

Haiti or the most densely Indian-populated parts of Guatemala, where the treatment of disease is still not far removed
from magic; and there is no particular reason to believe that
the situation will rapidly change.

In the same way there is an immense work to be done in
providing facilities for the care of the sick; the hospital
facilities available are in most of the states totally inadequate. In the United States there is one hospital bed for
every 10.7 persons out of 1000. This, of course, must be
regarded as the very apex of well-being, from the point
of view of the care of disease in the New World. No
Latin-American country comes very near it, though the
figure for Uruguay is 7.1, and for Panama 6.5. But for the
rest of the Caribbean area the figures are as follows: for
Costa Rica, 4, for Cuba, 3.8, for Nicaragua, 2.2, for El
Salvador, 1.5, for Honduras, 1.3, for Guatemala, 1.2, for
the Dominican Republic, 0.6, and for Haiti, .04. As a matter of fact, of the various states that we have been considering, five come at the very bottom of the list, being
excelled in their misfortune in this regard only by Bolivia.
Such figures make it graphically clear how much there is
to be done before tolerable conditions exist, let alone the
attainment of a standard anything like the standard of the
most fortunate Latin-American states.

Closely connected with the question of medicine, and of
public health, is the question of nutrition. Were we to cite
statistics on this matter, we would again become aware of
what an immense gulf separates the people of the United
States from the people of most of the countries of the
Caribbean. But it will be sufficient to say that in order to
provide a really satisfactory diet for the peoples of these
little states an immense amount has to be done, that in
almost every one of them the diet of the ordinary worker,
or ordinary dweller on the land, is monotonous, unvaried,
and far from "balanced," to use the favorite word of the

experts on this subject today. Here again there is much progress that must be made before really good conditions can be established.

There is always a danger, in such matters, that one will get from conditions in such striking contrast with those of the United States a point of view too deeply pessimistic. Nothing that has just been said should suggest for a moment that the populations of the Caribbean live in a condition so abject that nothing can be done about it. There is nothing to suggest that nothing is being done about it. The leaders of opinion in most of the countries concerned are well aware of the magnitude of their problems, and there is an increasing demand that these problems be faced. The proper attitude to take is not that of a kind of bleak pessimism, but rather a clear-eyed realization of the magnitude of the tasks ahead, and of the necessity of their being performed. But on this side of the matter we shall have more to say when we come to the relations of the Caribbean states with the United States and to the evolution of the good-neighbor policy.

There must, however, be no misunderstanding on one point. When it was indicated earlier in this chapter that the general state of education in most of the Caribbean countries is far from satisfactory, it must not be taken for granted that this implies a low state of culture throughout every class in the community. No error is commoner, and none more gross, than that contained in the assumption that there is no cultivated class, and no cultural achievement, in the states of the Caribbean. The exact reverse is true. Almost every one of the republics has produced persons of genuine intellectual distinction in many phases of human activity; and there is every reason to admire the cultural level which has been achieved by important elements in most of these states.

Take, for example, the republic of Cuba. Despite the

venality of much of the press, there is in Cuba at least one great newspaper, the *Diario de la Marina*, which, in the opinion of a competent judge, "in its coverage of foreign news, its editorials, its special articles, and its literary supplement, ranks far ahead of the majority of papers in the United States." There is in the field of literature such an important figure as Jorge Manach. There is a widespread interest in music, a creditable philharmonic orchestra in Havana, and some important work in the field of composition by such men as Lecuona. There is a school of modern painting, which, while not so impressive as that of Mexico, is yet worth noting. There is in the field of history such a distinguished figure as Carlos Trelles, in the field of international law such an outstanding personality as Bustamante, in the field of medicine such a well-known personality as the present president of the republic. It would be easy to lengthen the list, but enough has been said to make it clear that we do not need to regard the Cuban republic as by any means devoid of intellectual and artistic distinction.

What is true of Cuba, moreover, is true, though perhaps in less striking degree, of most of the other states. Haiti, it is commonly assumed, is the most backward. Yet Haiti has produced a poet of real tenderness and distinction in Oswald Durand, who writes in the Creole language of the country, and a distinguished historian and student of his own people in M. Jean Price-Mars. Or, again, let us look for a moment at the Dominican Republic. Probably the most distinguished student of Latin-American literature is the Dominican Pedro Henriques Ureña, while the names of such men as Fabio Fiallo and Amerigo Lugo are well known throughout the whole of the southern continent. Or take again the case of Nicaragua. Perhaps the most influential of all Latin-American literary men of modern times was Ruben Darío, who was a citizen of this republic, and whose work profoundly affected numberless other important figures in the intellectual history of the Americas. Or take, still again, Costa Rica. The *Reportorio Americano*, which began its existence at San José a quarter of a century ago, and has long been under the editorship of Joaquín Garcia Monge, has been well described as "a tribune of the social and political problems of all Hispanic America." Such a list as the above might be lengthened indefinitely; there is not a single one of the Caribbean republics which cannot point to some figure of distinction.

Nor should one imagine that it is only in the literary field that there are indications of a vivid culture. In the field of music Cuba, as already indicated, is undoubtedly a leader; but there is among the educated classes in the Caribbean countries an appreciation of music that is certainly no less widespread and profound than that which exists in the United States. Architecturally, too, the spirit of the Caribbean peoples has expressed itself in more than one distinguished public building, in the magnificent capital at Havana, in the modernistic buildings of the Nicaraguan capital, in the private houses of the newest section of Guatemala City. In painting, too, there are important figures, men like Arrúa and Vides in El Salvador, or Pacheco, Amighetti, and Dego (this last a caricaturist), in Costa Rica. It would serve no useful purpose to weary the reader with an extended list of such figures; but it ought emphatically to be understood that the aesthetic side of life is by no means neglected.

In addition to the work of the more sophisticated, moreover, there exists in many of the Caribbean republics a folk art that has a charm of its own. The Creole songs and stories of the Haitian peasant have a simplicity and charm that gives them a distinction of their own. And in the sophisticated society of today, there is, indeed, a special attraction in the sense of beauty displayed by simple and naïve people in simple and naïve ways. The *huipiles*, or *overgarments*, woven by the Indian women of Guatemala, are becoming better and better known for the beauty of their coloring and the unique quality of their design. The folk music of the island of Cuba has been winning for itself a special place of its own, somewhat akin to that of our own spirituals. We shall be very wrong if we fail to take note of these developments.

There is one final aspect of the life of the people of the Caribbean that we must notice for a moment when we consider the texture of their society. That is the aspect of religion. And here the range is much greater than one would at first suppose. It is true, of course, that all of these countries are Catholic. But in most of them, the Church struggles against much indifferentism, against vulgar superstition, and against its own poverty in numbers as in resources. In the republic of Haiti, for example, there were in 1944 only 205 priests (all but 8 of them foreigners) in a population of over two and a half million. The work of these men, it is true, was supported by the religious orders, and the number of Brothers and Sisters in the country amounted to 471. But such a small group cannot possibly carry on a truly effective work, even through the small mission chapels which are scattered all over the country. Nor is it to be said of the Haitian elite that they form, on the whole, a particularly devout class. Indeed, the plain fact of the matter is that the folk-religion of Vodun, or Vaudoo, as it is sometimes called, plays fully as great a part in the life of Haiti as does formal Christianity. This amazing cult, which has often been misrepresented by travelers to Haiti, and of which the most gory and exaggerated stories have been told, is in reality a kind of naïve polytheism, based on a belief in all sorts of gods and spirits, and upon the belief that these spirits can enter into or "mount" the individual, can effect cures of disease, and can bring good and evil fortune in their train. There seems little

BETWEEN
THE
AMERICAS

ALASKA

CANADA   LABRADOR

UNITED

STATES

*Area included in the
end paper map*

MEXICO   CUBA   DOM. REP.
                                            P.R.
               BR. HON.   HAITI
               HONDURAS
GUATEMALA   NICARAGUA   LEEWARD
EL SALVADOR   IS.
     COSTA   PANAMA
     RICA   VENEZUELA   BR. GUIANA
                                              D. GUIANA
               COLOMBIA   FR. GUIANA

ECUADOR

                               BRAZIL

                       PERU

                               BOLIVIA

APPROXIMATE   PARAGUAY
POPULATION
    IN
MILLIONS
(Independent areas only)

                      CHILE
                                    URUGUAY

               ARGENTINA

Country	Population
Panama	0.6
Costa Rica	0.7
Nicaragua	1.0
Paraguay	1.1
Honduras	1.2
El Salvador	1.9
Dom. Rep.	1.9
Uruguay	2.2
Haiti	2.7
Ecuador	3.2
Guatemala	3.5
Bolivia	3.8
Venezuela	4.2
Cuba	5.0
Chile	5.3
Peru	7.9
Colombia	10.3
Canada	11.5
Argentina	14.1
Mexico	19.6
Brazil	41.5
United States	141.0

doubt that, so far as the masses are concerned, this body of belief is at least as influential as formal Christianity. It is not, as some ignorant travelers have suggested, particularly brutal, or bloodthirsty; but it does, of course, reflect a cultural situation that is certainly not that of distinctively Christian states.

The situation which exists in Haiti can be paralleled, in a sense, with that which exists among the Indian population of Guatemala. Nominally, of course, these people are Catholic. But their faith is hardly more than a veneer, and since the confiscation of Church property under Barrios it has been difficult to maintain a priesthood at all adequate to provide for their religious needs. Rude idols can easily be seen by the visitor to the tourist city of Chichicastenango, and at Momostenango, not so far away, the people still practice rites that go back to the days before the Conquest, and invoke the favor of deities who have been worshiped for centuries. The churches themselves are often unmanned, or are in the hands of *confradías*, or associations of believers, who use them in a manner hardly conformable with Christian orthodoxy.

The cases of Haiti and of Guatemala are, perhaps, as extreme as can be found. But the role of the Church in most of the countries of the Caribbean has been a restricted one, largely on account of government policy. Rarely does a Caribbean government contribute effectively to its support. In the Dominican Republic, for example, only a few years ago there were but sixty priests for a population of at least a million and a half. In Costa Rica, the wealthiest of the Central American states, the Church is almost equally poor, and there are but one hundred and fifty priests in the whole country. The situation is much the same in the other republics, and is, one imagines, likely to remain so. Most observers of the scene in general seem to feel that there has been a distinct decline in religious intensity among the

Caribbean peoples, and that the position of religion is less secure than it was fifty or a hundred years ago. And nowhere does the Church occupy that favored position that might enable it to recoup its losses, and play a larger part in the life of the community.

In so stating the matter, we must beware, however, of seeing the matter in terms of black and white. The consolations of faith, the moral influence of belief, the pure aesthetic satisfactions that flow from the beautiful ritual of Catholic Christianity, all of these can be found in every one of the republics. Everywhere a minority, at least, in the cities perhaps much more than a minority, is sustained and strengthened by religion. And everywhere, today, as it has always been, men and women draw inspiration for the good life from the teachings of the priesthood. The Church is not so powerful as it once was; but its influence cannot be, and ought not be, entirely disregarded.

Is it possible that there is a place in the Caribbean states today for the gospel of Protestantism? The question is sometimes asked, and ought to be candidly answered. And the answer of most of those who know best the temperament of the Caribbean peoples would certainly be in the negative. The Latin nations, for reasons that doubtless lie deep in the national psychologies, have never been attracted to the reforming sects. Nowhere does such a faith seem to make much headway; and, indeed, it is sometimes rather more irritating than helpful, so far as the general intercourse of the United States with the neighbor republics is concerned. It does not provide, at any rate, a major solution of any of their problems, and can hardly be expected to succeed on any important scale.

What is to be said by way of summary with regard to the peoples of the Caribbean? Certainly there are many problems to be solved. Certainly, there is much to be done in the field of education, in the field of public health, in many other spheres of action. But there is no reason why one should be appalled by the magnitude of the task, or why one should give way to a sterile pessimism. The states of Central America, and of the Caribbean in general, have made a very notable advancement as compared with their situation a hundred years ago. There is no reason why this advance should not continue. There is no reason, in an age of social consciousness, why the same forces that are operating in other parts of the world should not operate here. Indeed, we have already seen that they do so operate. But the task ahead is one which depends, in no small measure, upon the attitude and the policies of the great nation of the North, with which all of these republics are in intimate relations. It is time that we should turn to an analysis of the place of the United States in the affairs of the Caribbean.

5. The United States and the Caribbean

The foreign policy of the United States, at the outset of its career as a nation, was largely concerned with two kinds of problems, the problems created by the French Revolutionary and Napoleonic Wars, and revolving around the question of neutrality, and the problems of territorial expansion on the American continent. But, in so far as American statesmen looked outside their own borders, they very early began to think of the area of the Caribbean, and especially of the island of Cuba. As early as 1809, for example, Thomas Jefferson, whose idealism was united with a remarkable acquisitive instinct where the interests of his country were concerned, spoke of Cuba as an interesting addition to our Federal Union. Fourteen years later, at a time when there were many rumors of European intervention in New World affairs, and much suspicion of European purposes, John Quincy Adams, then Secretary of State, wrote a famous dispatch to Erving, our minister in Spain, in which he clearly laid down the principle that the United States could not see with indifference the transfer of the island from Spain to any other power. Such declarations, in diplomatic business, are very likely to conceal a more positive interest on the part of those who enunciate them. The Adams declaration, indeed, was frequently reiterated by American Secretaries of State in the course of the next

thirty years, never with greater force than by Secretary
Edward Everett in 1850. And, in addition to this, the
United States on more than one occasion raised the question of the purchase of Cuba at Madrid. It did so, in the
first instance, as early as 1848; it did so again eleven years
later. And in the intervening period, in 1854, there occurred
the famous episode of the Ostend Manifesto, in which three
American diplomatic officers, meeting on European soil,
enunciated for the benefit of their own government the
remarkable proposition that Spain was under a moral obligation to sell her choicest possession in the New World,
and that if she refused to do so it would be time to consider whether measures ought to be taken to wrest it from
her. It is probable that had it not been for the slavery question (for Cuba was slaveholding territory in this period)
the territorial longings of the United States might have
found even more vigorous expression. It was the strong
opposition of the North to the extension of slave territory
that did much to render abortive any such project as the
one to which we have just alluded.

There was, however, one other aspect of Caribbean affairs that began to engage the attention of the American
government in the period before the Civil War. The idea
of the construction of an interoceanic canal either across
the Isthmus of Panama, or further north, across the territory
of Nicaragua, was almost as old as the discovery of the
Continent itself. But it was not until the 1830's and the
1840's that it began to be seriously considered, and to form
the subject of inevitable diplomatic discussions on the part
of the United States. Thus, in the year 1846, the American
government signed with the government of New Granada,
then in possession of the Isthmus of Panama, a so-called
treaty of guarantee, by which it assumed obligations to
maintain uninterrupted transit across the Isthmus. In the
same period, it began to reveal for the first time an interest

in Central America, in which the British were carrying on what to Washington appeared to be unseemly diplomatic activities. And out of the diplomatic wrangling which ensued there finally came the Clayton-Bulwer treaty of 1850, by which the British and American governments agreed to share in the responsibilities incident to the construction of an interoceanic canal. The Clayton-Bulwer treaty was followed by more discussion, and by a decade of constant controversy, but we can say with some assurance that by the time of the Civil War American interest in the idea of trans-isthmian communication had been vigorously manifested, and registered in a solemn international compact.

The years after the close of the great sectional conflict saw a new interest in the Caribbean. William H. Seward, expansionist by temperament, attempted in 1867 to acquire the Danish West Indies for the United States, as a convenient coaling station for our vessels; Grant, in his Presidency, embarked upon a fantastic scheme for the annexation of the Dominican Republic. But in neither one case nor the other was American public opinion ripe for a policy of acquisition; the treaty with Denmark slumbered in the Committee on Foreign Relations of the Senate; the Dominican project, in spite of all that Presidential pressure could do to push it through, was defeated in a decisive vote, in which leading Republicans, such as Charles Sumner, opposed the President. And though the awakening interest in the navy in the 1880's led to the discussion of various schemes for coaling stations, of which perhaps the most significant was for a station at the Môle St. Nicholas, in the island of Haiti, no actual acquisitions of territory took place down to the year 1898. But despite this fact the interest in the island of Cuba continued; in the long Cuban insurrection which began in 1868, and extended over almost a decade, there was much sympathy for the insurgents manifested in the United States; and when a new revolt broke forth in 1895, the same thing was true. At the same time American politicians and publicists showed a change of attitude with regard to the canal question. President Hayes, as early as 1879, made it clear that the United States believed that it must alone construct and control an interoceanic canal; and there was, on the basis of this point of view, an increasing demand for the abrogation of our pact with Britain. In this, as in other matters, the keen observer of American politics in the 1880's and early 1890's might have seen signs of a new assertiveness on the part of the United States; but it was not until almost the end of the decade that events took place which were to reshape American policy in more than one respect, and decisively influence the attitude of the United States towards the affairs of the Caribbean.

Among the problems that must always puzzle the historian is the problem of changes in the national mood. Yet such a thing as the national mood may surely be said to exist. At times a nation may seem to withdraw within itself; at other times it seems to seek a larger role and a wider influence. The period from 1865 to 1895 in American diplomatic history is on the whole a period in which the American people had little interest in foreign affairs, and little desire for adventure or expansion; yet in the course of it there can be seen developing new forces and new outlooks which were to produce a kind of American imperialism. On the naval side this new temper was represented by Alfred Thayer Mahan, whose classical treatments of the importance of sea power suggested inevitably a policy of acquisitiveness on the part of the United States; on the political side it was represented by such men as Theodore Roosevelt and Henry Cabot Lodge, who were young enough to have no sentimental aversion to war based on the holocaust of 1861–1865, and whose self-confidence and pride in America were not untouched with a kind of jingoism. Politicians and navalists, however, did not stand alone; there were academicians like John W. Burgess; there were clergymen like Josiah Strong; there were newspapermen like Hearst and Pulitzer. Whether these men evoked or reflected a changing temper it is hard to say; but at any rate the temper was there, and a kind of crusading ardor, mingled with a comprehensible impatience at the incredible incompetence and brutality of Spanish rule in Cuba, and crystallized by the famous episode of the *Maine*, brought the country in 1898 into the briefest, but certainly not the least important, of its wars.

The conflict with Spain produced, of course, a new balance of power in the Caribbean; it resulted in the liberation of Cuba (which after a brief occupation, was given its independence in 1902), and in the American acquisition of the important island of Puerto Rico; and among the strategic changes which took place at its end one of the most important was the right conceded to the United States by the Cuban government to a naval base at Guantánamo, on the south coast of the island. Very obviously, the war stimulated among American naval men a new interest in the area; it stimulated also the growth of the navy itself; and in the next decade and a half considerations that had seemed relatively unimportant in the nineteenth century began to bulk large in the minds of many Americans interested in the problems of sea power. Moreover, the war tremendously increased the interest in the canal problem, and it was, indeed, within a few years, followed by decisive developments from this point of view. The long voyage of the *Oregon* around Cape Horn to join Admiral Sampson's squadron before Santiago dramatized to the mass of Americans the significance of a short route of communications between the two oceans; and American diplomacy lost no time in preparing the way for the consummation of a long-cherished idea. It was not difficult to persuade Great Britain, isolated in Europe, and farsightedly pursuing a policy of rapprochement with the United States, to consent to the abrogation of the Clayton-Bulwer treaty, and even to agree, albeit reluctantly, to the American fortification of the projected canal; and on the heels of this success the administration of Theodore Roosevelt sought an understanding with Colombia for the construction across the Isthmus of Panama of the necessary waterway. There followed an episode which is not the most satisfying to Americans who wish to see their country observe the highest standards of international conduct; for when the Colombian Senate rejected the agreement which had been negotiated at Washington the Roosevelt administration adopted a course of action which was to expose it to severe criticism. It did not, as has sometimes been charged, instigate revolution on the Isthmus, but when a revolutionary movement broke out there, it sent naval vessels to Colón, landed troops which barred the way to Colombian forces which might conceivably have suppressed, or attempted to suppress, the revolution, recognized with a haste that many persons thought indecent the new government that was formed at Panama, and speedily negotiated with it a treaty which provided for the construction of the canal. Its conduct on this occasion long poisoned American relations with Colombia, and was not without effect in other parts of the American continent; partial amends were made for it by a treaty with Colombia nineteen years later. But, however doubtful the methods employed, the results of the episode just mentioned were that the canal was begun, and in 1914 it was opened to traffic for the commerce of the whole world.

In the construction of the canal we can find the solidest reasons for other developments in American policy in the first decade of the twentieth century; here was a great new line of communication in which the United States had a paramount and fundamental interest; and the increasing sensitiveness of the American government with regard to the situation in the Caribbean, and the increasing stress it laid on noninterference by European powers in the area, must both be considered as intimately related to the problems of the defense. Thus, there was quite a flurry in 1900 when rumors arose of the intention of Germany to acquire the Danish West Indies; solemn warning came from Elihu Root, then Secretary of War, against any such project; and two years later our government negotiated a treaty with Denmark for the acquisition of the islands, a treaty, which, unfortunately, failed of ratification at Copenhagen. In the same way public opinion became very restive when in 1902 Great Britain, Germany, and Italy attempted a punitive blockade of Venezuela; the resentment at the use of force by Europeans so close to the American zone of special interest was far greater than it had been on any previous occasion. And, more important still, the touchiness which these two incidents illustrate was translated into a new maxim of American policy, into the so-called Roosevelt corollary to the Monroe Doctrine. In 1904 President Theodore Roosevelt laid down this significant proposition; that, in its own interest, the United States might be compelled to intervene in the affairs of Latin-American states in order to prevent intervention by others, and that it would undertake such intervention as a logical application of the Monroe Doctrine; and as a measure justified by the necessity of keeping European powers aloof. Before long what had been enunciated as theory was in a modified form translated into practice; in 1905 the administration, being confronted with the possibility of European interference in the affairs of the disorderly Dominican Republic, negotiated with the government of that country an arrangement for the collection of the customs by American officers, and this agreement was translated into a treaty in the same year.

At the same time the Roosevelt administration began to

take an interest in the region of Central America. For the most part, outside of negotiations relating to the canal project, our relations with these states had been anything but close; but the growth of American financial interests there, together with the increasing strategic significance of the area, produced a decided change in attitude. The United States bestirred itself for the first time to put an end to the disastrous internecine conflicts which had so often bedeviled the politics of the Isthmus, and in 1907 at a Conference in Washington a series of agreements were drawn up, looking to the settlement of disputes between the Central American states through an International Court of Justice to be established at Cartago, and adopting other agreements which were intended to produce tranquillity. The state of Honduras, the battleground of many of these conflicts, was internationalized; and it was agreed that the contracting parties should not allow political leaders from a neighboring state to live near the border of the country whose peace they might disturb, and that they should arrest and bring to trial any person who should attempt to stir up insurrection against another republic. Most important of all it was provided that recognition should be withheld from governments that came into power by revolutionary means.

In addition to all these things, the Roosevelt administration found itself obliged actually to intervene in the most important of the Caribbean states. It had withdrawn from Cuba, as we have said, in 1902, leaving a native government behind it; but the withdrawal had not been wholly without condition. The so-called Platt amendment, which was incorporated both in the Cuban constitution, and in an international treaty, permitted the United States to reoccupy the island in case such action were necessary "for the preservation of Cuban independence, the maintenance of a government adequate for the protection of life, property and individual liberty." In the elections of 1905 a critical situation arose; the reëlection of Estrada Palma was contested by dissentient elements; a short time after the reinauguration of the president revolt broke out, and though the American commissioners sent to Cuba made a sincere effort to settle the difficult problems that had arisen in a spirit of compromise, they were unable to do so. With the deliberate intention of bringing about intervention, indeed, the president and the vice-president resigned; Cuba was literally left without a government, and accordingly there seemed to be no other course than for the Americans to come in. The second occupation was thus begun in the fall of 1906; it lasted for about two years and three months; it ended with the holding of a fair and free election, and with the handing back of the government to the Cubans in the winter of 1909.

The mounting interest in the Caribbean area which became so marked with the Roosevelt administration has from that time forward remained and inevitably remained undiminished. The sea itself had become the focus of the lines of international trade; the canal was a fundamental American interest; the economic influence of the United States in the region steadily increased. Indifference in such circumstances was impossible; but it is fair to say that there was little uniformity of policy in dealing with the states of the area in the twenty-four years between Theodore Roosevelt and the New Deal. To understand the period at all, we must look at our relations with various states in turn.

In Cuba, the most important of the republics of the Caribbean, there was, after 1906, no actual intervention in the literal sense of the word. The Taft administration, whose Secretary of State was Philander C. Knox, a statesman distinguished for his limited knowledge of the psychology of the Latin-American mind, constantly made suggestions to the Cuban government as to the conduct of its affairs, and attempted to an unusual degree to regulate the political morality of the young republic. It expressed itself, for example, on the question of amnesty after the Negro revolt of 1912, on a contract for the improvement of the harbors of the island, on a concession for the reclamation of the vast Zapata swamp. Viewed abstractly, its point of view may not have been without some justification; but viewed concretely, there can be little question that this kind of meddling was not calculated to improve the relations or strengthen the bonds between Cuba and the United States. The Wilson administration was somewhat more circumspect, and did not arrogate to itself so remarkable a concern for the virtue of the Cuban people. When in 1916 President Menocal was reëlected in a campaign conspicuous for the truly magnificent scale on which electoral corruption was practiced, and when an insurrection broke out in consequence, the United States gave no encouragement to the insurgents, and acted on the principle that it would not go behind the returns. In 1920, it acted somewhat differently, sending observers to the island who watched over the presidential election of that year, and following up this action by dispatching General Crowder to Havana to settle the electoral disputes that arose in the wake of the campaign, and to arrange for new elections in about a fifth of the voting districts. But these steps were, at least on the face of things, requested by the Cubans themselves, and cannot be regarded as an officious interference in the affairs of the republic.

Far different was the situation under President Harding. The economic situation in the island at the end of World War I soon became a serious one. The end of the year 1920 had seen the collapse of sugar prices, and a state of virtual prostration. The budget was badly unbalanced, and the government was compelled to default on the bonded debt. The regime of President Zayas was in a desperate situation, from which it could only extricate itself by a new loan in New York. Taking advantage of these circumstances, the American government, through General Crowder, exerted a very sharp pressure on the Cubans to make what it regarded as the necessary reforms. Indeed, for a brief period, the American envoy became the virtual dictator of policy. But his rule did not last long. No sooner was the loan obtained by the president of Cuba than the measures that had been adopted were whittled down or set aside, the so-called "Honest Cabinet," whose composition Crowder had dictated, was dismissed from office, and the normal course of Cuban political life resumed.

Perhaps the disillusionment caused in Washington by the promptitude with which the reforms of the Crowder era were put aside explains the policy of indifference that followed. There never was a worse government in Cuba than that which succeeded General Zayas. Gerardo Machado is the most sinister figure in Cuban history. He began not unpromisingly, but as time went on he suppressed all opposition, consolidated the various political parties behind him by terrorism and corruption, and established the only truly dictatorial regime in Cuban history. The United States under Hoover and Coolidge abstained from all interference with, and all condemnation of, this odious regime. When in 1931 an abortive revolt broke out, the neutrality of the United States was strictly enforced against the insurgents. The principle of noninterference was carried to its very fullest extent, and to the critic of the Washington government it seemed as if the United States were prepared to tolerate any regime so long as it was not hostile to American interests.

Yet the same administration which observed the establishment of tyranny in Cuba with complacency dealt perhaps the heaviest blow that has ever been dealt to the prosperity of the island. In a period of depression, when in any case the fall in the price of world commodities would have affected Cuba most unfavorably, the administration encouraged the enactment of the Hawley-Smoot bill, which raised the duty on Cuban sugar to a new high. The depth of the depression in Cuba in 1931 and 1932 is by no means unrelated to American policy. We acted, indeed, in these years, with a callous disregard of the interests of our neighbor state, and indeed of the interests of the United States itself. There is not a more glaring example of the unhappy indirect consequences of protectionism on a friendly state than the bill to which we have just alluded. Policies such as this can do damage little less, perhaps even greater, than any resort to physical coercion.

It is difficult, as will have been made clear from what has just been written, to summarize our Cuban policy in the period we are examining. It was certainly not extraordinarily harsh or domineering; but it was often futile in its interferences, and very rarely constructive in any broad sense of the term. Under Knox Cuban political morality came in for our severe strictures; under Hoover a situation far more serious was tolerated without the slightest difficulty. It would be difficult to find a coherent principle which would serve as a key to the American attitude in the twenty-four years that extend from the exit of the first Roosevelt from office to the advent of the second.

In Central America the Roosevelt administration had laid the foundations of a new policy, aimed at keeping the peace of the Isthmus, at maintaining international peace among the states of the Isthmus, and at discouraging revolution. Here, as in Cuba, Secretary Knox demonstrated an uncanny genius for the wrong approach. His attempt to extend the Roosevelt policy of customs control over Honduras and Nicaragua failed in the case of the first-named state, and resulted, as we shall see later, in intervention in the second. Nor was the Wilson administration wholly fortunate in this part of the world in raising the prestige of the United States. It entered into a treaty with the Nicaraguan government providing for the construction of an interoceanic canal by way of the San Juan River, and for the establishment of a naval base on the Bay of Fonseca. Its action was challenged by both Costa Rica and El Salvador, on the grounds that their interests were affected in these respective regions. These two states appealed to the Court of International Justice; but the United States and Nicaragua both insisted that the case did not come under the Court's jurisdiction, and refused to have anything to do with its deliberations. The position thus assumed dealt a deathblow to this new tribunal, and did nothing, one may be sure, to raise American prestige in Central America. Nonetheless, it is fair to say, all the Central American states but El Salvador, bound to the United States as they were by important economic interests, followed the American government into the war against Germany in 1917.

In the years after the peace of Versailles there were again signs of instability in the region of the Isthmus. Remarkable peace had reigned there ever since the overthrow of the Nicaraguan trouble-maker Zelaya in 1909; it was highly desirable that this peace should continue. The United States took the lead in the promotion of a conference which met at Washington in 1923. Once again a pledge was made not to recognize governments which came into power through a *coup d'état* or revolution, "so long as the freely elected representatives of the people thereof have not constitutionally reorganized the country," and, above and beyond this, the signers of this agreement went on to declare that in no case would they recognize any government whose head was closely connected with the leaders of the revolution. Of this technique of nonrecognition it will be better to speak in more detail in a later chapter; but it is interesting to observe that it represented a method of approach to the problem of internal stability and international peace which has rarely been applied in any other area, and which has, in no other case, been actually incorporated in solemn international agreements. Thus our Central American policy has a character of its own.

So, too, has our policy in Panama. In the period we are considering, there was often in our relations with this little state a degree of intimacy and a variety of issues that give them a special interest. In the period down to 1917, there was frequent supervision of elections, though with the consent and indeed at the invitation of the Panamanians themselves. In the years following World War I, Panama appointed an American financial adviser or fiscal agent, who carried through an effective program of financial reform, extending over a number of years. Important questions involving the interests and the protection of the Zone were solved by the closest coöperation between the two governments; the question of proper measures of sanitation, for example, was settled in constructive fashion by conceding to the American authorities power to take adequate preventive measures in the Panamanian cities of Panama and Colón; important problems of defense were settled by the grant of the Panamanian government of the right to construct and operate radio stations in Panamanian territory, and later by partial American control of private aviation; the reorganization of the Panamanian police was undertaken under the direction of an American army officer. Many of these measures were the result of accords freely entered into, but on occasion the United States acted vigorously, and in a more coercive spirit. In 1918 it stationed some of its troops in the province of Chiriqui, and there they remained for some time. On at least two occasions it threatened to take over the policing of Panama City and of Colón if conditions there did not improve. In 1921 it brought strong pressure on the Panamanian government to accept an arbitral award fixing the boundary between Panama and Costa Rica. Such measures, however, were certainly not without substantial justification; and, on the whole, it may be said that in our relations with this little state in the quarter of a century under review the United States showed restraint and wisdom.

In Cuba sporadic intermeddling; in Central America a new policy of nonrecognition; in Panama friendly and invited supervision tapering off as the period lengthens; these are some of the elements in our Caribbean policy in the years 1909–1919. But the most interesting and the most controversial we have as yet barely touched upon, the policy of armed intervention, practiced in Nicaragua, in Haiti, and in the Dominican Republic.

This policy raises some fundamental and interesting questions, as to the relations of small states and great ones. To evaluate it as correctly as we can is the necessary prelude to our analysis of the contemporary era. Let us then go back for a little to discover its origins, and to see how it came about that in the years from 1912 to 1934 American marines were encamped upon the soil of three independent states, and the United States involved in a policy which had portentous consequences in the field of international relations.

Marxist writers on American foreign affairs have no difficulty in this, as in other matters, in finding a simple explanation of what actually occurred. To them the occupation of Nicaragua, of the Dominican Republic, and of Haiti is a simple example of financial imperialism. The United States intervened in the affairs of all these states for the protection of the always sinister interests of American capital; it acted, as countries of satiated capitalism always act, for the promotion and extension of its own economic interests. Such an interpretation, of course, has the virtue of simplicity; but, like most simple explanations of human events, it is by no means adequate or accurate, and it does not correspond with the facts. It would be nearer the truth to say that the initiative for such a policy came, not from private interests bent on gain, but from government officials who were more concerned with strategic and political than economic facts; and that American finance in coöperation with these officials was, of course, led on by the hope of gain, but by a hope infinitely less potent and intense than led it to other kinds of adventure, and to other activities outside the United States.

We have already noted that in the administration of Theodore Roosevelt there developed an increasing sensitiveness with regard to the area of the Caribbean; that this sensitiveness translated itself into a new policy, the so-called Roosevelt corollary to the Monroe Doctrine; and that the assertion of the necessity for the United States to exercise an international police power was based upon the fear (whether justified or not) that European states might take advantage of domestic disorder and financial irresponsibility in the Caribbean to establish themselves upon American soil. In the Roosevelt administration the Caribbean was in process of becoming what it is in effect today, an American lake, and it was government, not private enterprise, which was primarily interested in this process.

When the Roosevelt administration went out of office in 1909, and was succeeded by that of William Howard Taft, Philander C. Knox became Secretary of State, and he attempted, as he himself would have declared, at any rate, to carry further the policies of the previous administration. He envisioned American action to restore the finances of some of the republics of the Caribbean; he thought that the transfer of their indebtedness from European (mostly English) to American hands would reduce the dangers of foreign intermeddling; and he recognized that in order to carry out such a policy, and in order to induce American bankers to participate in such a program, it was necessary to assure them of the safety of their operations by reserving to the United States the right of intervention in the affairs of the republics whose fiscal affairs were to be reorganized. He argued, no doubt, that the control of Dominican customs by the United States under the agreements of 1905 and 1907 had been a distinguished success (and so indeed it looked at the time); and that the extension of such a system could work nothing but good both to the beneficent guardian and to the wards of that guardian.

Unhappily, the methods by which Secretary Knox sought to carry out his policy were heavy-handed in the extreme, as is best illustrated in the case of Nicaragua. In 1909 the ruler of this state was that same Zelaya of whom mention has more than once already been made. Zelaya had not endeared himself to American interests in the republic, or indeed to any of those who wished to see tranquillity in Central America. A revolution broke out against him in which the hand of certain American business concerns was clearly to be discerned. The dictator resigned, and in his place a member of his own, Liberal, party was chosen president. But Secretary Knox was led to continue his support of the insurrectionists even after Zelaya's withdrawal; American vessels were sent to Greytown, on the east coast of Nicaragua; and the upshot of the matter is that, as a result of American partiality, the Conservatives came into power. With the regime thus established Mr. Knox proceeded to negotiate a treaty calling for the control of the customs, and conceding a right of intervention; and without waiting for the ratification of this treaty by the Senate of the United States he persuaded certain New York bankers to make loans to the new government. This hasty and ill-advised action won him no friends on Capitol Hill, as was intelligible enough, and the convention with Nicaragua could not be pried out of the Foreign Relations Committee for some time. In the meantime one difficulty after another assailed the new administration in Nicaragua; it was threatened with revolt, not unnaturally, since in all probability it had never commanded the allegiance of the majority of the people; and in 1912 American marines were landed to keep in power an unpopular regime. Apart from any other consideration the administration felt under obligation to protect the interests of the bankers whom it had induced to lend their money to the Nicaraguan government.

The marines were to remain there until 1925. In that year an attempt was made to put an end to the Nicaraguan affair, but the attempt was unsuccessful. Hardly were the marines withdrawn than a revolution took place, and a government under General Chamorro was elected to power. This new regime was, in due course, forced out of office by the attitude of the American government; but President Diaz, who was chosen as Chamorro's successor, soon found himself confronted with civil war. A violent struggle began in which Diaz's opponents seem to have received some assistance from Mexico. Secretary Kellogg's excited imagination soon found in the events in Nicaragua a danger of Bolshevism, and in due course marines were landed, ostensibly for the protection of American interests. The occupation thus effected was followed by the snuffing out of resistance, and by an American mission which laid plans for a fair election in 1928. This election took place as scheduled, and the marines were again withdrawn in 1929.

Just as Mr. Knox was responsible for the intervention in Nicaragua, so, too, he laid the foundations for intervention in Haiti. There he was unable to proceed so far, or to embroil matters so thoroughly, but in persuading the National City Bank of New York to take a part of the stock of the Haitian Bank he again put the State Department in the position where it was bound to feel obligated to support an American financial interest. At the moment nothing very significant occurred; but Haiti sank into a condition of chronic disorder in the succeeding years, which naturally jeopardized the position of the Bank, and which constituted an a priori argument for intervention. In the meantime other developments were taking place which looked in the same direction. In the State Department, among those influential but little known subordinate officials who often have so much to do with the formulation of policy, the idea appears to have developed that it would be useful to establish a far-reaching measure of control over the island republics of Haiti and the Dominican Republic, measures which would include customs administration, the creation of a native constabulary officered by American marines, and perhaps complete supervision of the internal finances of these two governments. The disorder which existed in both of the countries concerned was, at this time, indeed extreme, and offered some excuse for action, and for the gratification of the American propensity to "tidy things up," as imperialist Americans often put it; and in addition to this, in the case of Haiti, the administration was no doubt made a bit nervous by French and German proposals in the summer of 1914 for the joint control and administration of the customs. But the successive presidents of Haiti, who rapidly succeeded one another in this period, showed a natural reluctance to subject their country to external control; and the attempts to persuade them to accept voluntarily the beneficent ideas of the State Department were unsuccessful. In the summer of 1915 a particularly outrageous situation provided the justification for action. In the course of the revolutionary disturbances that convulsed the republic a Haitian president who had been driven from office and who had sought refuge in the French legation was forcibly seized, dismembered, and his mutilated body paraded through the streets of Port-au-Prince; the result was the landing of American marines. Thus came a second intervention.

In the case of the Dominican Republic the course of events was as follows. The first few years of the agreement of 1907 were thoroughly satisfactory. But, after the death of President Cáceres in 1911, the country began to sink into graver and graver disorder. The State Department, once again under the influence of a theory of action which was never publicly discussed, and which had no deep roots in American opinion, attempted to persuade the Dominican government of President Jimenez to accept proposals similar to those which had been pressed upon Haiti; the president could not see his way to do so; and, finally, faced with foreign pressure and with the threat of domestic revolt, he resigned. The country was left temporarily without a government, and in this emergency the American marines appeared. They landed at Santo Domingo City in the summer of 1916. Thus came a third intervention.

These three intrusions on the territory of independent states, it should next be noted, though similar in some respects, did not, as a practical matter, run precisely the same course. In Nicaragua, for example, the government in power was left to administer affairs, and the American marines performed the function of making a return of the Liberal party to power difficult, if not impossible. But elections were held at the intervals stipulated by the Nicaraguan constitution, and interference with the existing regime was limited to measures of a financial character. Thus the customs administration was put under American control; when the American bankers required further security for the loans which they had made, the state railway of Nicaragua was placed in their hands; there was a certain amount of supervision over internal expenditures; but with these significant exceptions, and always remembering that the presence of the marines very distinctly cramped the style of the political opposition, the government of the country was still in native hands. In Haiti, to take our second case of intervention, another type of machinery was set up; the national legislature was dissolved, but the national executive remained, and so, too, did an appointive body which participated in the legislative process, and which was known as the Council of State. In the case of the black republic the measures of supervision were far more sweeping; the creation of a constabulary, which came, in the case of Nicaragua, only after the second intervention in 1927, was in this case undertaken from the first; extensive measures were set on foot for the improvement of the public health; a road-building program was inaugurated; the financial administration was almost entirely in American hands. In the third instance, that of the Dominican Republic, matters went even further; the native government was entirely suppressed, and a military government set up under the Navy Department in Washington; besides the constabulary, as in Haiti, and the road-building program, there was also an ambitious scheme of public education; all these, of course, in addition to the inevitable financial control. In all three interventions, of course, the United States, during the period of intervention, called the tune, and in all three cases it maintained its troops on foreign soil against the will of the inhabitants of the countries concerned.

It would be useless to deny that in every one of these instances some very substantial achievements have to be set down to the credit of the Americans. In each case, for example, the reorganization of the finances of the republics concerned was carried through on an efficient basis; not only was the way prepared for the service of the public debt, but proper measures were taken for the adjudication, and, inevitably, the scaling down of the foreign claims against the governments. It no doubt means more to foreign investors than it does to the Haitian peasant, or the Nicaraguan coffee-worker, or the laborer on the sugar plantations of the Dominican Republic, that since the interventions the public debt has been, with only minor exceptions, regularly paid. But it can hardly be denied that a good credit standing is closely related to the development of the Caribbean states, and that the United States has effectively assisted them in attaining such a standing.

In Haiti and the Dominican Republic important road-building programs were undertaken during the occupations. Better communications, as we have already seen, must inevitably play a substantial part in the improvement of economic life; and in both of the instances cited the change under American rule was important. Haiti, in 1915, had virtually no roads passable for motor traffic. Today it has a network which effectively serves every part of the republic. Its neighbor state was slightly better off. But the improvement of the years 1916–1924 was substantial; indeed one may say fundamental.

In the Dominican Republic the school system was completely reorganized with the aid of a commission of prominent Dominicans, and the number of children enrolled was increased from 18,000 to nearly 100,000 with a great improvement in the daily attendance. In Haiti a Central School of Agriculture was established near Port-au-Prince to assist in a program for the improvement of agricultural conditions, and to provide teachers for the rural schools. Here the success was certainly far less spectacular than at the other end of the island. The recruiting of teachers was from the beginning very difficult; the peasant class itself was too backward to provide personnel; and the members of the elite who were persuaded to participate in the program were often indifferent to the problems of agriculture, and by no means free from prejudice or snobbery in their dealing with the masses. But it may reasonably be assumed that the effort was not entirely wasted, and it has, indeed, been continued in the period since the American withdrawal.

In Haiti important steps were taken to deal with the problems of public health. American naval doctors set to work energetically to deal with the medical scourges of the island, and they set up free clinics in many parts of the republic. Effective work was carried on in the Haitian towns, by the institution of street-cleaning services, establishment of good water systems, and the control of the mosquito. Hospitals were built, and medical inspection of school children developed. A parallel program, though hardly an ambitious one, was carried through in the Dominican Republic. And in both cases it may fairly be said that the results achieved carried over into the period of restored independence.

Finally, in all three cases, the interventions ended with the establishment of a reasonably well-equipped and well-disciplined police force, or constabulary. Such a force presented, no doubt, a danger; for the commander of the constabulary might, and in some striking instances did, use the guard as a stepping stone to political power. But, on the other hand, the maintenance of domestic order has an undeniable importance in any civilized state, and the equipment and training of a reasonably responsible force, with a morale of its own, was at least a protection against the constant cycle of revolutionary violence, pointless and wholly indefensible, such as beset the Haitians, for example, in the years from 1910 to 1915. The task remains of subjecting such a force to the civil power; that task is not fulfilled; but we may still hope that the institution of the constabulary will, in the long run, turn out to be among the constructive achievements of the American occupation.

Nonetheless, the interventions had another side, and a far less attractive one. In the first place, they were deeply resented by the peoples concerned. In Nicaragua, during the early period, the country was quiet. But at the time of the second occupation the United States was not so fortunate. A guerrilla leader, Sandino by name, refused to accept the agreement by which the Nicaraguan factions, under American leadership, prepared the way for an honest and orderly election in 1929. Retiring to the north of the country Sandino engaged in raids which were always annoying and sometimes tragic, and in July of 1929 he wiped out an American garrison and a Nicaraguan guard unit at a place called Ocotal. It cannot be said that he secured widespread support, even from the Nicaraguans themselves. But his resistance was embarrassing, and it was naturally made the basis for a constant agitation abroad against the imperialist United States.

Far more significant were the difficulties met with in the Dominican Republic and in Haiti. In the first of these two countries there was a good deal of resistance to the occupation, and though it was easy to describe those who engaged in it as "bandits," to the naïve Dominicans they often appeared in the guise of patriots. The military government was compelled to carry on fairly extensive operations in 1917 and 1918, especially in Seibo and Macoris provinces; and in addition to this it was led, perhaps not always without some color of reason, into acts of repression which had repercussions far beyond the island of Santo Domingo. In particular, its trial of the Dominican poet, Fabio Fiallo, for some not very incendiary remarks about the occupation, resounded throughout Latin America, and did little to increase the prestige of the United States. Inevitably, too, under circumstances of guerrilla warfare, some acts of violence were committed by American marines which had no justification by any military code; and these acts, exaggerated and inflated by the opponents of the intervention, naturally put the American government in an unenviable light in the forum of Latin-American opinion.

What was true in the Dominican Republic was true, a fortiori, in Haiti. There an attempt to revive the institution of the corvée, or of forced labor, was the greatest factor in producing what can hardly be otherwise described than as an armed revolt against American rule. The disaffected among the Haitian politicians naturally did all that they could to foment the uprising, and the Haitians found a leader of some capacity in one Charlemagne Péralte. They were, of course, no match for the American marines in open combat. But they carried on a guerrilla warfare which took two years of military operations to suppress, and which resulted in the killing of something in the neighborhood of 1500 Haitians. And, as in the other end of the island, the circumstances of the conflict inevitably led to individual acts of brutality which were given an exaggerated importance in the critical press, and which could hardly fail to provoke widespread resentment. Curiously enough, neither the Haitians nor the Dominicans seemed to enjoy unreservedly being civilized from the outside; and this strange preference of theirs for conducting their own affairs in their own way was a circumstance of which, in the long run, the American people were bound to take note.

For the undoubted fact of the matter with regard to the people of the United States is this. They have had their imperialistic moments. They are not exempt from the passion for remaking the world in their own image, and of correcting the obvious weaknesses of others. But, in the main, they do not like, and sooner or later even react against, the coercion of other peoples. We are not to suppose that at any time a nation-wide indignation resulted from these acts of the United States; but it is fair to say that interference in the affairs of independent states never commanded the united enthusiasm of the citizens of this country.

If the interventions of the period 1912–1934 were unpopular among certain sectors of opinion in the United States, they were still more unpopular among Latin Americans. In many ways the Wilson administration had sought wisely and successfully to woo Latin-American opinion; but its action in the Caribbean operated in no small degree to offset its sagacious policy in Mexico, and its general sympathies with the states to the south. By the end of Woodrow Wilson's term of office, the American government had a distinctly bad press in more than one Latin-American country, and at the Santiago conference in 1923, in the Harding years, the hostility of much Latin-American opinion to this country was undisguised. Very hard-boiled people might say that this did not matter, that we could afford to regard with contemptuous indifference the point of view of our neighbors; but only very hard-boiled people would take this point of view. For apart from any other considerations the good will of the Latin American might be of value from a purely economic point of view, while their political sympathy with the United States might also be useful in the event of such complications as those from which, in 1920, the United States had just emerged. And, finally, Americans *do* think of foreign policy in terms of idealism, as well as in practical terms. The interference of the American government in the Caribbean ran counter to a deep-seated and widely held conviction that there was something about such interference incompatible with the professed standards of conduct of the great American democracy.

There was still another thing to be said. It needed only a superficial knowledge of conditions in such a state as Haiti to recognize that the establishment of genuinely democratic institutions, imposed from above, was to all intents and purposes an impossible task. The Occupation might seek to lay the foundations of economic progress and of ordered peace; but it could by no means guarantee, in twenty years or even in thirty, forty, or fifty years, that on these foundations a democratic government could be built. In the last analysis the form of a people's institutions must depend upon that people itself; popular rule, by very definition, could not be successfully imposed; were it to come at all, it would have to come by a slow evolution. Why, then, in the face of severe criticism both at home and abroad, commit oneself to an endless supervision of the affairs of another state? Why, indeed?

Finally, it might well have been said that one of the principal reasons for the interventions no longer existed as time went on. The policy of the United States in the Caribbean had been dictated in part by strategic motives; it had been geared to certain conceptions of national defense. But the defeat of Germany for a time removed all sense of danger; and in the twenties, and the first years of the thirties, before Hitlerism had begun to throw its baleful shadow over the whole world, the necessity for occupying the islands of the Caribbean was by no means apparent. It was natural, then, that the mood which dictated the interventions should give way to another; and that by an evolution which ripened into clear and definite policy, the period of tutelage should give way to another, to the period of the "good neighbor." This great and important change, which forms or at any rate should form the basis of present action, we must describe in the next chapter.

6. The Good-Neighbor Policy—Political

The foundation of our relations with the states of the Caribbean area during the last thirteen years has been the policy of the good neighbor. This policy has won for the United States, not only in the Caribbean, but elsewhere, an admiration and regard that is beyond question; and it represents, indeed, a remarkable development of international relations in general. For it is founded on complete respect on the part of the strong for the rights and independence of the weak; on coöperation, not on tutelage; on hope, not on fear. It is a policy which has both its political and its economic aspects. On the political side its guiding principle is nonintervention; on the economic side its essence consists in the encouragement of freer trade relations, in the stimulation of the economic well-being of the states to the south of us, as a matter of international concern, and of progress for the whole world, and in the development of that expanding economy on which the welfare of humanity so largely depends. The understanding of this policy is central to an understanding of our position in the Caribbean, and, indeed, in the western hemisphere in general.

Let us look first at the good-neighbor policy from the political point of view. Interference in the affairs of the independent states of the New World by the American government, as has already been said, had never been truly popular in the United States. The Roosevelt corollary to the Monroe Doctrine had met with much criticism at the time of its pronouncement; and its first practical application, the establishment of the customs control in the Dominican Republic, had been opposed by a large section of the Democratic party. It is, of course, possible to attribute this to mere partisan feeling; but even partisans do not oppose unless they feel that they have something to gain by opposing, and it may be fairly assumed that the Democrats, in taking the position that they did, were conscious of the support of a substantial body of American opinion. In the same way, the opposition in the Senate had taken their stand against the Knox treaties of 1911 with Nicaragua and Honduras; and the failure of these treaties certainly indicates that there was no enthusiastic body of public opinion behind the policy of financial tutelage. On the whole, the increasing measure of control that was exercised in the Caribbean area in the first and second decades of the twentieth century was a matter of State Department policy, rather than of popular desire; and perhaps it could not have been carried through at all had it not been for the fact that at its apogee American public opinion was much engrossed in the problems of World War I.

At any rate, no sooner was that war over and a Presidential campaign set afoot, than an issue was once more made of our Caribbean policy; Senator Harding, in the electoral contest of 1920, found himself much concerned, at least from the angle of partisan oratory, with the sad plight of the Dominicans and the Haitians. It does not really matter whether Senator Harding was sincere or not; whether he had any exact or precise notions of what Haitians and Dominicans were like or not; whether he was well or ill informed. He was raising the issue because, like the practiced politician that he was, he was aware of the American repugnance to whatever savored of bullying a smaller people; he was speaking to the authentic American conscience. The plain fact of the matter is (and we all ought to take pride in it) that as a people we are by no means naturally disposed to the domination of others; our instinct, sometimes falsified in action, but always deeply felt, is to wish to see our own democratic principles translated into reality elsewhere. This was true in 1920; and it is true today.

The reaction against the policy of the interventions was not slow in showing itself after the end of that war; when the Harding administration actually came into power, it set in motion, under the distinguished leadership of Secretary Hughes, the process of withdrawal from two of the three countries that we had occupied a few years before. In the case of the Dominican Republic, indeed, this withdrawal was completed before the next election. Mr. Sumner Welles was sent to the island to negotiate the terms of the evacuation, and after months of patient and delicate negotiation the way was found, first to set up a provisional government, and then to provide for an election and the choice by the Dominicans of a permanent regime. By the summer of 1924 the American marines had been withdrawn, and the Dominicans embarked once more upon the dangerous but inspiring course of national independence. One mark of tutelage, and one mark only, remained; the customs of the island were left under American administration, and the customs system set up under the American occupation was, so it was stipulated, not to be changed in certain essential respects.

The Harding-Coolidge administration not only liquidated the Dominican intervention but also attempted to bring the occupation of Nicaragua to a close; and a few months after President Coolidge began his elective term the marines withdrew from Managua. But in this case, as we have seen, events did not follow so smooth a course, and within two years the United States had intervened again. There was certainly much criticism of this second intervention; the justification that was offered of it, that there was a danger of Bolshevist influence in Central America, seemed to many persons to border on the absurd; and the Democrats in Congress attempted to make partisan capital out of the attitude of the administration. As a matter of fact, the Coolidge administration in this matter was distinctively on the defensive, and it soon recognized the fact. Henry L. Stimson was sent to Nicaragua to prepare the way for an honest election, and for the installation of a regime honestly chosen to assume power, and by 1929 the marines had been once more withdrawn.

In the meantime there were many signs that public opinion in the United States was reacting against the policies of supervision and of interference that had so often characterized the relations of the American government with the states of the Caribbean. Nor was it only public opinion in the United States that began to express itself. When the Fifth Pan-American Conference met at Havana in the summer of 1928, nothing was more remarkable about it than the almost universal unpopularity of the United States. The administration called from retirement the most respected of all Republicans, Charles Evans Hughes, to justify its attitude; but the states of Latin America displayed a hostility to American policy that it was beyond the power of this eminent American statesman to exorcise. Never before had this country been so thoroughly on the defensive at a Pan-American gathering; and while Mr. Hughes, with legalistic acumen, attempted to defend a doctrine of "interposition" as distinguished from "intervention," he found himself in a distinctly embarrassing position. At Havana it became clear that the United States might choose two paths in its relations with the states of the New World, the path of friendship or the path of domination.

The lesson of Havana was not lost on American politicians. It was a fact of some significance that in 1929, when the Kellogg pact for the renunciation of war was presented to the Senate for ratification, the Senate Committee on Foreign Relations, in reporting it for approval, submitted also a memorandum on the Monroe Doctrine, in which, among other things, the Roosevelt corollary was explicitly and distinctly disavowed; and this gloss on the famous Doctrine was approved by the Senate itself. In the State Department, too, a new spirit made itself manifest; in 1930 the Department published a running commentary on the Monroe Doctrine that was known as the Clark memorandum; and here again the Roosevelt corollary was ruled out of the account. In other words, both the Senate and the principal executive agency of the government concerned with foreign affairs had now retreated from the position assumed by Theodore Roosevelt a quarter of a century before. Nor is it to be omitted from consideration that the Hoover administration, which took office in 1929, began negotiations for American withdrawal from Haiti, the last of the states of the Caribbean to remain under American tutelage.

It was, however, under President Franklin D. Roosevelt that the attitude towards the states of Latin America was clearly and precisely defined, and became known, in due course, as the policy of the good neighbor. The phrase had been used by the President in his inaugural address, and at the time had no restricted application, but was merely an expression of a general point of view. But it was repeated by Mr. Roosevelt in a speech which he made on Pan-American Day, in 1933, and before long it came to be associated with American policy towards the states of the New World. It expressed in a nutshell what was the aspiration of the United States; but it needed years of laborious effort to translate it into a living reality, and the necessity for constant reaffirmation of its spirit will last, one might almost say, as long as the republic itself.

The first opportunity for the Roosevelt administration to

demonstrate its attitude came in connection with the affairs of Cuba. There, in the summer of 1933, the government of President Machado, which, as we have seen, was the most ruthless and brutal in the history of the Cuban republic, was becoming more and more inured to the methods of dictatorship. The economic situation was almost unrelievedly bad. The popular discontent had for some time been showing itself in acts of individual violence against the members of the Machado regime. The Hoover administration had stood by supinely, while conditions went from bad to worse. Its successor was not content to do so. Utterly repudiating the notion of forcible intervention, it took the view that the time had come to attempt to assist the Cuban people in some constitutional and orderly solution of its growing difficulties, and in the spring of 1933 Mr. Sumner Welles, who had already had wide experience in dealing with Latin-American peoples, and who, it will be remembered, had presided over the elaborate negotiations which preceded American withdrawal from the soil of the Dominican Republic, was sent to Havana.

It was the purpose of Mr. Welles to bring about by negotiation between the president and the opposition groups the withdrawal of the president from power. The administration and the opposition proved willing to accept his mediation. But before positive results were secured, a mutiny of the Cuban army took place, and Machado was forced to flee. A provisional regime under Dr. Carlos Manuel de Céspedes followed.

The government that was formed in August 1933 was not, however, of long duration. At the beginning of September there occurred another mutiny in the army, under the leadership of that brilliant figure, Fulgencio Batista, who, later, as we have seen, became president of Cuba. The political leadership, in the confused conditions that then arose, came into the hands of Dr. Ramon Grau San Martín,

the present president of the republic. The new government
acted as, and indeed was, very much a government of the
Left. If purely material considerations had controlled American policy, in the conditions which existed in the fall of
1933, it would have been extremely easy, under the Platt
amendment, to have found justification for intervention. The
situation was very serious. Sporadic rebellions broke out in
various parts of the republic, and a condition of virtual
anarchy existed. An administration less farsighted, or more
subservient to the pressure of special interests, would probably have yielded to the temptation to restore order by
forcible means. Not so the administration of President Roosevelt. In an extremely trying situation it held its hand, with
what results will shortly appear.

The administration of Grau San Martín was not recognized by the American government. This fact has, on occasion, been made a matter of reproach by American critics.
It has been contended that while there was no physical
intervention there was exerted a moral pressure which was
hardly less objectionable, and which derogated from the
right of the Cuban people to determine their own destiny.
But there is most certainly another side to the case, and it has
been stated by Mr. Welles. "None of the established political parties, none of the commercial or business interests, no
responsible labor organization, and only a few of the members of the professional classes supported the government,"
he declares. "I have always felt," he was to write at a later
date, "that in view of the existence at that time of the
Treaty of 1901, which granted this government the right of
intervention in Cuba, and only because of that fact, the
United States would have been derelict in its obligations to
the Cuban people themselves had it given official support to
a de facto regime which, in its considered judgment, was not
approved by the great majority of the Cuban people, and
which had shown itself so disastrously incompetent in every

branch of public administration." For so long as the treaty containing the so-called "Platt Amendment" continued in force, the Cuban people were persuaded that recognition of a government by the United States was tantamount to official American support for that government.

Whether this view be fully accepted or not, it is certain that the Grau San Martín regime proved extremely short-lived, and was overthrown by the Cuban people themselves. In January of 1934 a new turn of the political wheel occurred. Grau San Martín, amidst a howling throng of his partisans, embarked for Mexico, and a well-known and highly respected Cuban, Carlos Mendieta, succeeded to the presidency. The new government was speedily recognized by Washington; and what was more important negotiations were soon entered into which resulted in the abrogation of the Platt Amendment, and in the voluntary renunciation by the United States of its right to intervene in Cuba. When has a great power ever shown a more generous and forbearing attitude than the United States showed in connection with the events that we have just outlined?

But before the abrogation of the Platt Amendment, events had occurred on a wider stage which accentuated and gave a more general character to the policy of the good neighbor. We have already seen that throughout Latin America there was increasing dislike of the policy of intervention that had been practiced by the United States. The matter had been discussed at Havana; but there, largely owing to the position assumed by the American representative, no action had been taken. There was, by now, no doubt of either the theory or the desire of the other American republics; what they desired, and what they had made clear that they desired at Havana, was a definite incorporation of the principle of nonintervention into a convention, which should, to all intents and purposes, be declaratory of the American law of nations. And the opportunity for attaining this objective came with the Pan-American conference which met at Montevideo in the fall of 1933. There the United States, under the leadership of Cordell Hull, was to make a vital contribution to the cause of international understanding, and to carry forward in the most striking fashion the policy of the good neighbor.

The proposal which came before the conference was phrased in extremely broad terms. It was a part of a projected convention on the Rights and Duties of States. It read as follows: "No state has a right to intervene in the internal or external affairs of another," and, obviously, represented an immensely significant decision. It is not strange that the American delegation viewed so sweeping a statement of the law with some misgiving, and that in accepting it Secretary Hull stated that the United States reserved its rights as by "the law of nations generally recognized." But accept it he did, nonetheless. It is doubtful if on any previous occasion a great state has made a more dramatic and a more unselfish gesture in the interests of international understanding. If, in the long run, discussion and the force of world opinion are to regulate international affairs, the more powerful governments of the world will have to act frequently in the spirit in which the United States acted at Montevideo.

The convention which was signed at Montevideo was ratified by the Senate of the United States without a single dissenting vote. Such action was impressive evidence of the manner in which American public opinion reacted to the doctrine of nonintervention. It furthermore underlined the fact that the policy of the good neighbor was not a partisan policy of a Democratic administration, but a national policy to which all elements in the country were committed. The direction of American diplomacy had been set; it remained to follow steadfastly along the course.

In the year 1934, as we have already seen, the United States, of its own free will, gave up the Platt Amendment.

In the same year it withdrew its forces from the soil of Haiti, though it retained a measure of control over the customs. And in the same year it began negotiations with the republic of Panama that culminated in the treaty of 1936. By this important compact, which was finally concluded only after months of patient negotiation, Panama agreed, as partner of the United States, to take whatever measures might be necessary for the protection and defense of the Canal, and for its efficient maintenance and operation. The right of intervention in Panama, conceded by the treaty of 1903, was renounced. A large number of outstanding problems, which had long needed to be liquidated, were settled by supplementary agreements, which did justice to the views of the Panaman state, and improved its economic situation. The "good-neighbor" policy was thus being most effectively applied in practice in negotiations with individual states.

Towards the end of the year 1936 another important step was taken. At the suggestion of the President of the United States the Argentine government called a conference to meet at Buenos Aires to consider the best ways of maintaining the peace of the Western hemisphere, and safeguarding its future security. And at this conference the bases of the good-neighbor policy were affirmed and extended. On the one hand, the principle of nonintervention, accepted by the conference of Montevideo, was reasserted in terms even more specific than those of three years before. And it was furthermore provided that if any question arose as to the interpretation of the article in which the principle of nonintervention was laid down, resort should be had to the procedure of conciliation or arbitration or judicial settlement for the solution of the matter. This time the United States made no reservation whatever to the convention; and thus it again accepted, and this time accepted unequivocally, the most far-reaching restraint on its own physical power, and dedicated itself to the peaceful solution of controversies with other states of the New World.

But it went further than this. It was able, at Buenos Aires, to secure the acceptance by the states of Latin America of the principle of consultation in the event that the peace of the American republics was threatened by a non-American power. And what is particularly interesting with regard to this agreement is that it was supported with the greatest warmth by some of the states of the Caribbean. Indeed, the Central American delegations wished to go further, and to declare that all of the American nations should "consider as an attack upon themselves individually an attack which may be made by any nation upon the rights of another." It was not possible, it is true, to secure the acceptance of this proposition in the form in which it was put forward, but on the other hand the Declaration actually accepted at Buenos Aires stated that "each act susceptible of disturbing the peace of the Americas affects each and every one of them, and justifies the initiation of the procedure of consultation." By the good-neighbor policy the United States was drawing together the states of the New World in common antagonism to the threat which was developing across the Atlantic.

A new step in the process was taken at Lima at the end of 1938. The Convention of Buenos Aires, while providing for consultation, had not established any machinery by which such consultation might be initiated. This omission was remedied by the Conference which met at Lima, and it was provided that the meetings of the foreign ministers of the various states might take place on the call of any one of them. And at Lima, as at Buenos Aires, in the carrying out of its program the United States met with very effective support indeed from the states of the Caribbean. Indeed, it is fair to say that no Latin-American republic responded more cordially to the efforts of the United States to attain hemispheric solidarity than did those with which we are specially concerned in this study.

The close association of the Caribbean states with the United States was only strengthened by the events of the first years of World War II. We may pass lightly over the Conference of Panama, which, occurring in the fall of 1939, was held under circumstances which still made it possible to believe that the New World would not be directly endangered by the war in Europe. But we can hardly deal so briefly with the course of events in 1940. For the German conquest of France in the spring of that year created an entirely new situation, and raised in direct form the question of the defense of the American hemisphere. The famous agreement by which the United States transferred to the British fifty over-age destroyers, in exchange for the right to establish bases on the British islands of the Caribbean, was the product of this period. But from the viewpoint of the good-neighbor policy the outstanding fact is the Conference of Havana. There the epochal declaration was made that "any attempt on the part of a non-American state against the integrity or inviolability of the territory, the sovereignty or the political independence of an American state shall be considered as an act of aggression against the States which sign this declaration." And, in addition to this, the machinery was provided whereby, if there appeared to be any danger that European possessions in the Caribbean might fall into the hands of Germany, the American nations might step in and set up a regime of provisional administration, conceived on broad lines, and thoroughly regardful of the rights of the inhabitants of these territories. It is a matter of significance that these agreements were signed in the capital of Cuba. The success of any conference can be much affected by the diplomatic atmosphere in which it takes place. And the achievements of the Conference of Havana bear a direct relationship to the strong feeling of the Caribbean states that in this international crisis they should coöperate to the full with the United States.

The policy of the "good neighbor," in its relation to the Caribbean, was again affirmed when in December 1941 the Japanese launched their attack upon Pearl Harbor. Almost immediately, and in advance of a general Pan-American Conference held at Rio de Janeiro, the states of Central America and the republics of the Caribbean declared war on the Axis. The very countries which had been the "victims" of American intervention, or which had observed that intervention at close range, now spontaneously and instantly aligned themselves with the United States. A more striking vindication of the wisdom of the Roosevelt administration could hardly have been imagined. And in the years that followed, the good faith, the loyalty, and the effective economic aid of these states in their relation to the United States cannot be too much praised.

This chapter concerns itself with politics, and not with economics. For the moment, therefore, we shall not deal with those problems of trade and finance that became more and more significant with the actual coming of the war. The political problems of these years were naturally not particularly difficult. In the Grand Alliance that had been created for the defeat of the totalitarian powers, the states of the Caribbean stood ranged with the United States in intimate union. And by the Declaration of Washington, signed at that capital on the second of January 1942, they pledged themselves not to make peace separately but to remain united to the end of the war. The success of American policy was thus triumphantly affirmed.

Viewed in the perspective of the years which we have just traversed, the good-neighbor policy appears a distinguished success, on the political side, and was, as we shall see, a distinguished success on the economic side. And if we are to understand it in relation to the future we must ask some questions here with regard to the very bases upon which it rests.

In the first place, is the United States wise in pledging itself, as it has pledged itself, to complete abstinence from the use of force in dealing with the states of the New World? Is such an act of abnegation reasonable? Does it not go further than it is wise to go? Suppose, for example, a full-fledged Communist regime should some day be established in Cuba, a regime which definitely asserted its acceptance of the Communist faith, and which formed close relations with the U.S.S.R.? Or suppose, to take a case at the other extreme (and we cheerfully admit that these are extreme presuppositions and extreme cases), that there was established in one of the states of Central America a truly Fascist administration, which suppressed all public liberties, embarked upon a systematic program of Fascist instruction, and proceeded to raise and equip an army with a view to the conquest of neighbor states? In cases such as these, could the United States stand idly by, and watch the establishment in the New World, and not so far from its own shores, of governments whose principles it detested, and whose practical policies it could not fail to oppose?

No doubt in such circumstances there would be those who would not wish to press the principle of nonintervention to this, its absolute conclusion. A thoroughly Communist regime in Cuba would, in practice, not only involve American property interests to a very substantial degree; but it would also present a very definite threat to the security of the United States itself. It might well be used as a center for espionage in time of peace, and of espionage and sabotage in time of war. It would undeniably place problems of defense in a new context, and it would provide encouragement for those who seek to undermine that Pan-American solidarity which is, or at any rate ought to be, one of the objectives of American policy. It would be as foolish to view such a possibility with complete indifference as it would be to get the jitters about it before it was translated into reality. In the same way, a thoroughly Fascist regime in, let us say, El Salvador or in the Dominican Republic, would not only jeopardize important material interests, but it would constitute a menace to peace that could not be disregarded. Principles, even the best of them, are not usually susceptible of absolutely unwavering application; and there can be no doubt that in such circumstances the American government would find itself sorely tempted.

But before we decide that in such instances we should have to abandon the nonintervention policy, there are several considerations that ought to be kept in mind. In the first place, such extreme cases as we have just mentioned are not at all likely to occur; as we have already seen, the constitution of society in the Caribbean states, the habits of their peoples, the temper of their opinion, make either one of these calamities mentioned above extremely unlikely. We can easily imagine social policies more advanced than many Americans would approve; we can easily imagine dictatorships more harsh and reactionary than any American would welcome. But so close are the ties between the states of the Caribbean and the United States, so intimate the economic bonds between these republics and our own, that the adoption of policies utterly at variance with American sentiment appears extremely unlikely, if not impossible.

In the second place, the proper policy with regard to the Caribbean ought to be such as to prevent any such developments as we have just suggested. It is the business of the United States to see to it that these republics enjoy the advantages of an expanding economy, that they are helped to a greater and greater degree of prosperity, that in all of them the condition of the masses is steadily improved; and that bit by bit the conditions are created in them which will lead in the direction, not of totalitarian dictatorship, but of liberal social democracy. There is no reason to regard such a goal as Utopian; and certainly there is no reason to assume that conditions sufficiently satisfactory cannot be created and maintained as to eliminate the danger of totalitarianism.

Finally in the extreme cases that have been propounded, there might be at least a possibility of collective action, and collective action at the instance of the Latin-American states themselves. It is true that during the past year an incident has occurred which casts doubts upon the possibility of such action. In February last, the Uruguayan government, perhaps at the instigation or with the encouragement of the government of the United States, brought forward a proposal for multilateral intervention against any government which showed a clear and marked hostility to the democratic ideal. This proposal, it must be candidly stated, was not received with enthusiasm by the members of the Pan-American family. It is not overstating the matter, indeed, to say that it met with a very chilly reception. But it does not follow that this would always or necessarily be true, in all sets of circumstances. The Uruguayan proposal, in the concrete, was directed against an American, not a European, power. The reaction might have been quite different if the threat with which it had dealt had come from overseas. Were it to be dramatized by some decisive event, especially by an event that looked to a new threat from the Old World against the liberties of the New, against the very principle of self-government, there is reason to believe that the reaction would be quite different from what it was to the proposal of Mr. Rodriguez Larreta. The chance, at any rate, of a collective policy would be good enough, in all probability, to justify a cautious attitude on the part of the United States, and to make desirable an effort to develop some common principles of action. Latin Americans do not want to be dominated; they wish, naturally enough, to play a part in the decisions on which common policy is to be based. Should we not, at least, give them an opportunity to do so in case any such problem arose? Would we not, indeed, be in a stronger position, if we acted under the pressure of a rising public opinion throughout the Americas than if we acted alone? Or might we not find, on the other hand, that the reaction against a Communist revolution would soon come within the affected state, especially in the Caribbean area where every republic is connected by such close economic bonds with the United States? Might we not confidently hope, on the basis of experience, indeed, that no government could long survive in this region which had not the confidence of Washington? Might we not, therefore, proceed circumspectly if the danger did appear?

In the meantime we may fairly say that as yet the peril is not imminent. And with regard to all changes of policy and government within more modest limits, we can and should be content to stand upon the pure doctrine of non-intervention to which we are pledged. Indeed, as the very core of that doctrine, a very wide latitude should be left to the individual states of the area to control their own affairs; it should not be expected of them that in every respect they conform to the pattern of conduct which seems proper to the citizens of the United States; their efforts to deal with their social and economic problems should be viewed sympathetically; their institutional forms should be left to them to develop in conformity with their national genius and with their national tradition. To such a point of view the American government is committed; to such a point of view, indeed, it is pledged by the solemn engagements of the convention of Montevideo.

Here, indeed, we come to an aspect of the general problem that deserves more consideration than we have yet given it. It was a remarkable act of abdication on the part of the

United States when it consented in a solemn international treaty to forego the use of force in relation to its neighbors; but the spirit of the good-neighbor policy, as we have just intimated, suggests something more. There are other modes of influencing events than by the imposition of physical force; and it still remains a question how far the American government may legitimately intervene, by other means, in the affairs of the independent states of the New World.

The question has been raised in connection with the recent course of events in the Argentine. What happens in that remote state may seem, at first blush, to have little to do with American policy in the Caribbean; but in reality what is involved is a question of principle, and may as readily concern one of our nearer neighbors as the remote republic of the south of South America.

If we are to understand this problem, we must briefly sketch its background. That the statesmen of the Argentine should be jealous of the United States, that they should be distrustful of its leadership, and disposed to seek to counterbalance its influence is not perhaps strange in a proud, sensitive, and growing nation. In the thirties and the forties the Argentine government often sought to thwart American purposes in the Conferences of all the Americas; and only reluctantly, and later than any other power, it broke relations with the Axis in the war of 1939–1945. Moreover, the actual course of Argentine politics has been for some time very far from reassuring. Powerful military elements have exercised a decisive influence on policy at least since the middle of 1943; and the *coup d'état* of June of that year which underlined their dominating role in Argentine politics was followed by the withdrawal of many (but not all) of the diplomatic representatives of the Latin-American states from Buenos Aires. Unhappily, in the months that followed, the United States made no genuine effort to act on the principles which were involved in the good-neighbor

policy. It avoided, and discouraged, such a meeting of foreign ministers as had given consistency to that policy; and,
by so doing, it roused a very considerable resentment in
more than one Latin-American chancellery. For a little, in
the first months of 1945, it found itself brought to a change
of attitude; and at the San Francisco conference of that
spring, largely owing to an increasing distaste for its policy
among other of the republics, it found itself compelled to
agree to the admission of the Argentine government to the
counsels of the nations, and to a participation in the drafting
of the United Nations Charter. But shortly after these events
the Washington administration reverted to its former stand;
and as the time came for an election of a president in the
Argentine the American minister at Buenos Aires took an
active part in rallying the democratic forces within that
country to oppose the existing regime, and to prevent the
election of the ambitious Colonel Perón, who represented
the militarists. There has rarely been, indeed, a more striking
case of intermeddling in the domestic affairs of another
state than that which the United States practiced in the
Argentine in the closing months of 1945.

If such action were justifiable in one case, it would, of
course, be justifiable in another; and so it is that in our
consideration of our relations with the Caribbean, and with
the evolution of the good-neighbor power, we are compelled to consider the propriety of such acts of moral intervention.

It is, of course, true that the United States has both an
interest and a moral bias with regard to the progress of
democracy in the world at large. None but the doctrinaire
imagines that democratic government is universally attain-
able in a limited period of time; or that it corresponds to the
genius or the traditions of every one of the peoples of the
world, or to their economic circumstances. But we do believe here in America that democracy is a form of govern-

ment which contributes both to internal stability and to international peace; that it has this great advantage over all other forms, that it rests in a wider degree than any other upon the processes of consent, as distinguished from the processes of coercion; that by the very diffusion of power that it implies it prevents ambitious and selfish men from shaping state policy towards sinister ends, as did Hitler and Mussolini in the period that is just past. It would be too much to say that democracies are in all circumstances and inherently peaceful; but it is certain that they give to those who value peace an opportunity to express their views, and make themselves felt, which may be denied to the subjects of a totalitarian state.

But as a question of practical politics, it is extremely doubtful whether the United States strengthens democracy in fact by active participation in the affairs of other states. Appeals from the outside by a government over the head of constituted authority in another country seem in general to have been unsuccessful in the past, and are likely to be unsuccessful in the future. In the precise case which we have just discussed, it seems at least as likely that the decided partisanship of Mr. Spruille Braden at Buenos Aires strengthened the forces of reaction, and contributed to the election of Colonel Perón as president as much as it contributed to the cause of his opponents. In days of intense nationalism, the attempt of one government to influence public opinion in another by this sort of tactic is likely to be futile, and is certain to be perilous. The very human instinct to desire to run one's affairs in one's own way is likely to prove stronger than any urge to democracy in general. Moral intervention, in other words, is extremely questionable as a basis of policy.

It may be said by the partisans of vigorous action for the promotion of the democratic ideal that the stake involved is tremendous, and that in such a cause it is necessary, perhaps imperative, to take some risks. But in answer to any such contention there are a good many solid considerations on the other side. For the achievement of democracy is essentially an evolutionary process, and one that cannot be imposed; it appears to be connected, as we have already said, with the wide diffusion of property and a rise in the standard of living of the masses; it requires for its growth a solid foundation on the educational and cultural side; and it may be discredited by ill-judged or premature action on the part of its own votaries. There has been, at times, on the part of the United States, with regard to other governments, in a solicitude for the maintenance of democratic ideas, a kind of nagging petulance that by no means produces a disposition to conform in those who are its victims. The communication of ideals, either by one individual to another, or by one state to another, is at all times a matter for the finest tact and the most delicate feeling; and while it would be foolish and extreme to declare that no effective influence can ever be exerted directly, it is nonetheless wise to count far more on the power of example than on the force of precept. The instinct to perceive the mote rather than the beam is as old as human nature itself. But it is a dangerous instinct, and one that ought, in one's own interest, to be controlled. The reaction of Latin-American opinion to our interventions, and the reversion to former habits of undemocratic rule that has followed upon these interventions in every instance, a reversion which is often given too little emphasis in analyses of these interventions, demonstrates to a striking degree that any policy of intermeddling is more likely to be self-defeating than successful, and that it is by other means that we must promote the progress of the New World towards the realization of our own way of life.

This is not to say, however, that we need make no distinction whatsoever between one state and another, between an odious tyranny and a regime which aims at the development of self-rule. It is not necessary, for example, to praise effusively in diplomatic speeches those whom at heart we thoroughly disapprove. It is not necessary to give to dictators of the Trujillo type the prestige that they are sure to derive from friendly gestures from Washington. It is not desirable to advance money to Caribbean rulers who are virtually certain to use it for their own aggrandizement, rather than for the advancement of the public welfare. It is not at all required by the good-neighbor policy that we make gifts or sales of arms and ammunition to those who are suppressing dissent, and governing by force. It is entirely proper for our representatives to state and restate their own faith in the democratic way of life. The thing to be avoided is any kind of action which may give to rulers of the reactionary type an opportunity to appeal to national pride against the interference of outsiders, and which rouses the sensitive pride of the Latin Americans in general and suggests in ourselves a sense of supercilious superiority. In international affairs, as indeed in personal relations, it is very difficult to wield effective influence if one assumes a holier-than-thou attitude, and suggests that what is necessary for others is to come up to the remarkably high standard that one has already attained for oneself. Let us, in foreign affairs as elsewhere, strive to preserve a sense of humor and proportion.

In connection with this general question of attitude there is one special question to which we may well devote particular attention. That is the matter of withholding recognition from governments which we disapprove or which have come into power through other than democratic means. This policy, as we have already briefly mentioned, was given a special application in Central America. It seemed at the outset attractive enough in principle; it was adopted with no other purpose than to preserve good order and international peace. But how did it work in practice?

Certainly not brilliantly, so far as the prevention of revolution was concerned. The treaty of 1907 was shortly followed by a revolution in Nicaragua, a revolution which, as we have seen, led to American intervention and again in 1919. In 1911 there was a revolution in Honduras. In 1917 a *golpe de cuartel* in Costa Rica. In 1921 there was revolution in Guatemala. In only one of these cases was the nonrecognition principle successfully applied. Nor can the treaties of 1923 be said to have worked much better. They did not destroy the revolutionary habit; they merely, for the most part, altered its technique. Moreover, they were completely defied by President Martínez of El Salvador, who came to office by a *coup d'état* in 1931. Far from rallying to the support of the agreement on this occasion, the other Central American governments showed a distinct distaste for any such course. Costa Rica officially denounced the compact of 1923 at the end of 1932. And it was not long before the whole project had to be abandoned.

It is no doubt difficult for Americans, with their natural instinct for orderly process, to sympathize with the tendency to appeal to physical force which has in some degree characterized, in the past, the history of so many of the Caribbean states. But it would be taking an extremely narrow and uncomprehending view of things to condemn unqualifiedly the revolutionary habit in the history of Latin America. One has only to think of the utterly ruthless and disgraceful character of the Machado regime in Cuba to realize that there may be circumstances where there is no other appeal against a brutal and immoral tyranny. Revolutions sometimes end odious regimes, if indeed they sometimes install them. Even when they ignore, or give mere lip service to constitutional forms, they may represent relief rather than oppression. To refuse to recognize governments which issue from them may be, on occasion, to strengthen a very undesirable status quo.

But one may go further than this in making, on the whole,

a critical judgment of the nonrecognition doctrine. It is fair to say that this doctrine is likely to lead either to futility or to actual intervention. In the case of El Salvador, for example, mentioned above, the position taken by the United States was entirely without effect. It does not add to the prestige of any government to say that it will not do something, and then to come around to doing it. A still more painful example of this same difficulty is to be found in the policy of the State Department towards Argentina. The effort to ignore the government of General Farrell, to boycott it diplomatically, an effort begun in 1944, broke down in 1945. In this case, indeed, the nonrecognition principle never commanded the unanimous adhesion of the states of Latin America, and the attempt to use it diminished, if it did not destroy, the chances of Pan-American unity. The striking of a high moral attitude, when one is not ready to carry it through into practice, is hardly the best diplomacy. It has been, at times, perhaps a rather distinctive failing of the policy of the United States.

On the other hand, we repeat, a policy of nonrecognition may lead on to intervention in one form or another. This is precisely what happened in the case of Mexico in the administration of President Wilson. When Wilson came into office in 1913, there had just occurred a *coup d'état* in Mexico which brought into power the blood-stained regime of one General Victoriano Huerta; and this regime, on the basis of its origin, the President refused to recognize. But almost inevitably he was led by his hostility to this regime into acts of partiality towards the anti-Huerta faction in the civil war; and, what was more important, he finally resorted to force against the Mexican dictator, which, whatever its technical justification, involved very serious risks of war. The occupation of Vera Cruz in 1914, in retaliation for General Huerta's refusal to salute the American flag and render due apology for the detention of American seamen, did not, in the upshot, produce an actual armed conflict, in part because of the skillful diplomacy of the Wilson administration; but had the leaders of American policy been less adroit in their methods, it might easily have done so; and had Huerta himself been able to rally the nation behind him, even the coolness and ingenuity of the authorities in Washington might not have availed.

Or take another case. The attempt to apply the nonrecognition principle in Nicaragua in 1925 did not prevent the development of a situation in which American marines actually intervened; in fact, in its effort to apply the principle of legality the Coolidge administration found itself actually involved in a Nicaraguan civil conflict. In refusing to recognize a revolutionary government, it got itself tied up in the niceties of Nicaraguan constitutional law, and ended by virtually imposing on the Nicaraguan people a regime whose popular support may have been doubtful. This whole episode, one may be sure, did not add to the prestige of the United States.

All in all, then, the use of recognition as a political weapon is, I think, to be deprecated. There are, or ought to be, simple tests which can be applied, and which raise no question of interference. The simplest of all, of course, is that proposed by the Mexican publicist, Genaro Estrada, and which is sometimes described as the Estrada doctrine. By this rule, any government which actually is in control of the country is to be acknowledged. There are eminent students of American foreign policy, eminent statesmen, indeed, who believe that this rule is adequate. But something more is demanded, or has been demanded, in the past by this country. It has been regarded as necessary that a government, before it is recognized, should be ready and willing to perform its international obligations. It is probably accurate to say that this is official policy today. There ought to be nothing invidious in such a principle; it should not be applied in such a niggling spirit as to make the recognition of a firmly established regime a matter of indefinite diplomatic haggling, and it should not open the door to moral intervention in a new form; but in some extreme instances it might be necessary to apply it. At any rate, it is fair to say that up to date the Estrada doctrine has not been accepted as the basis of American policy.

There is still another aspect of the good-neighbor policy on which it is necessary to dwell for a moment, and which is an essential part of its spirit. The very essence of the policy lies in the principle of consultation. The nations of the New World are, according to this view, to be treated not only as juridical, but as moral, equals. Policies which relate to this hemisphere are to be forged in common, and not imposed by the United States on the other members of the American community. By such means, and by such means alone, can the solidarity of the American republics be maintained. It must be admitted that this ideal has suffered some damage since the halcyon days at the beginning of the war. The tone of some American officials in dealing with the Latin-American states has not always been that of friendly counsel, but has been rather wounding to the pride of those concerned. The Argentine policy of the United States has certainly not commanded universal support from the rest of the American galaxy, or even from the republics of the Caribbean. The publication of the so-called Argentine Blue Book in February 1945, with its charges of Axis collaboration, on the verge of an Argentine election, by no means was received with unanimous enthusiasm by our neighbors, and among those who were least enthusiastic was Cuba. The refusal of the United States until recently to take part in an inter-American peace treaty, to which Argentina should be a party, or indeed to participate in a conference for such a treaty if Argentina were a member of that conference, has not been based on any principle of consultation, and does not represent the technique which ought to be associated with the policy of the good neighbor.

Of course we must be prepared, in this period after the war, for greater difficulties in maintaining Pan-American harmony than was the case in the years of the thirties and early forties. It can hardly be denied that the rise of Hitler, and the menace of Germany, exercised a solidifying influence on the states of the New World. The centrifugal tendencies that show themselves in diplomacy at the end of every war are likely to be present on this side of the Atlantic as well as the other. But these considerations do not, or at any rate ought not, to invalidate the good-neighbor policy itself. They make it more imperative, indeed, that in its attitude toward other American states the United States should exercise genuine forbearance, and manifest a genuine willingness to common counsel. Now and again there are disturbing signs in American foreign policy that the arrogance that comes so naturally to a great and victorious nation and that is so easily the fruit of power is not entirely absent in the conduct of the United States today. It is easy to talk of the policy of the good neighbor; it is becoming conventional to pay tribute to it; but to practice it requires not only vigilance but a genuine willingness to accept the conceptions of common action and free discussion on which it is based.

In the meantime, there is one hopeful aspect of the matter. The good-neighbor policy was adopted without partisanship; and it has been continued in a nonpartisan atmosphere. There has been, particularly on the side of politics, almost no criticism of its fundamental ideas; and such opposition as has been manifested to State Department policy in recent years has come more from those who feared that the policy was being jeopardized than from those who disapproved of it from the beginning. In the Caribbean area the old habit of constant intermeddling has been pretty well abandoned;

and while there have been differences of opinion between the United States and some of the republics of the region on this question or that, the general tone of international intercourse is certainly not an unhappy one. The questions of the future, however, are as much economic as political; and to them we must now turn.

7. The Good-Neighbor Policy– Economic

We have summarized in the immediately preceding pages the implications of the good-neighbor policy from the political point of view. We must now attempt what is fully as important, an analysis of that same policy from the economic angle. But before we do this, even though it appears to be out of place in a work concerned fundamentally with matters of foreign relations, we must say a word about the general economic tendencies of the United States in the post-war era. The subject is, in fact, by no means irrelevant, for practically speaking it is impossible to make a sharp distinction between domestic and foreign policy; the one reacts upon the other, and the line between them is often difficult to draw. Who can doubt, for example, that the depression of 1929 had far-reaching consequences beyond the boundaries of the United States; that the collapse in this country helped to precipitate economic decline elsewhere; that in turn this economic decline brought about the growth of an intense nationalism, and in Germany a crisis which greatly aided the rise of Hitler to power; that the process of recovery absorbed the energies of the democratic nations at a time when they ought to have been girding themselves against the aggressor; and that the Great Depression thus contributed in fundamental fashion to the coming of the Second World War itself? And on the basis of the train of circumstance just described who can doubt that the future of international relations depends in no small part upon the domestic policies of the United States in the period that lies ahead? In the spring of 1945 the writer of this little book traveled back to New York from the Conference of San Francisco with a distinguished Chilean publicist, a former president of the republic, and in the course of conversation this experienced man remarked, "Only be prosperous! The other problems will then be infinitely easier." There was great wisdom in this pronouncement, and, accordingly, it seems wholly justifiable to say a word about the future of the American economy before discussing the application of the good-neighbor policy in the past, and its implications for the future.

The essence of the matter is this. Viewed from the historical point of view, the people of the United States have believed that the mechanism of business was largely self-regulating. Throughout the nineteenth century they took the oscillations of their economy for granted; they believed that depressions contained their own cure; that a process of natural readjustment took place at such times, and out of this readjustment prosperity came once more into being. But the Great Depression of 1929 shook the faith of many people in this point of view; it was unprecedented in its extent and intensity; and no doubt the various rigidities introduced into the economic order by trade unions, trade associations, farm blocs, and other groups, made the process of recovery by deflation more and more difficult. There are still influential elements in the United States which cling to the doctrine of automatism; which have a congenital prejudice against any kind of economic planning; which contemplate with complacency in these days in which we live a boom followed by the inevitable recession. But there is a new gospel abroad in the economic world; and this gospel teaches that it is possible to preserve the economic machine in some kind of equilibrium, or even to contemplate a steady positive development. According to the growing and influential school of economists who take this point of view, the primary cause of depression is over-saving; in the natural operation of the economy there comes a time when there is no longer sufficient scope for the new capital that has accumulated to find profitable investment; and the funds that are thus built up, which are neither spent nor put to work, create a decline in consumption. This decline in consumption becomes progressive; as one industry after another finds its markets shrinking, still other sectors of the economy are affected, and in due course there is a serious economic debacle. Such a situation may not arise for some time; the discovery of new processes, the creation and satisfaction of new human wants, the growth of international trade, and many other factors, may for some time keep the economic machine in full motion; but nonetheless that machine has a tendency to come to rest; and when that tendency appears the way to depression is open. This, in short, is the fundamental hypothesis of the new economics; and on the basis of this hypothesis a new and positive program for the prevention of economic collapse has been formulated.

What, then, is the positive program put forward by the economists of the New School? Briefly, it is this. That when the economy shows signs of slowing down, "public investment" shall take the place of private investment; new roads will be built; new TVA's will be projected and carried through; new housing projects will be undertaken; and these various forms of activity, and of course many others, will be carried on to restore the equilibrium of the economy. All of them will in turn restimulate private enterprise, open up new areas to private capital, and pave the way for a return to prosperity. There is a difference of opinion among the economists as to how such a program shall be financed; a considerable group believe that taxes should be kept high in times of prosperity, permitting the reduction of the public debt, and that in periods of recession borrowing should be resorted to; some of them go further, and maintain that a steady and substantial increase in the public debt is not incompatible with the health of the economic body, and cite the experience of the past to show that this is true; and some, like Sir William Beveridge in his *Full Employment in Great Britain*, seem to believe that such a program can be largely financed, and ought to be financed, from taxation. But whatever the method to be employed, the general principle is fairly clear; it is that public spending, or public investment, as it is winningly called, should take the place of private investment when the economic machine shows signs of slowing down. The validity and the practicability of such a viewpoint remains to be proven by experience; one suspects so simple a remedy for so complex a phenomenon as the down turn of the business cycle; but, with all proper reservations, it may at least be said that it offers greater promise for the future than a blind faith in automatism, or acquiescence in the immense suffering that economic depression brings in its train. It implies for many economists, at least, the adoption of certain definite policies in a period of widespread employment such as lies immediately ahead; it suggests, for example, that in such periods there should be no sweeping reduction in taxation; and it suggests, too, some restraint in governmental spending since, in a period of prosperity, the effect of such spending is to raise the price level, increase the pressure on wage scales and prices, and make more difficult the smooth operation of the economic machine. But the real test of the New Economics will come, of course, when recession sets in, and perhaps as significant a question as can be posed today is as to whether when that time comes, the machinery of government will be in the hands of those who are ready to try to apply the new theories, or in the hands of those who will let economic disease spread, as the Hoover administration let it spread in 1930 and 1931.

It is not maintained, of course, that it is possible for the average American citizen to decide this question of the future at this precise moment; we cannot indeed foresee the circumstances under which he will need to decide it; but it is just as well for us all to realize that some time the decision must be made. No lover of international peace, no friend of progress, can fail to hope that when the time comes this country will be ready to meet the test in a fashion more constructive, and more bold, than that in which it met the Great Depression of 1929.

The hypothesis that we have just discussed has its application to foreign no less than to domestic affairs. In the long run, it is to the interest of the whole world that the states of Latin America shall undergo a healthful and progressive development. But such a development can hardly take place without some assistance from the outside, for reasons that have already been indicated. The formation of capital in most of these communities does not come about on a sufficient scale to provide for the optimum measure of growth. It will not, for some time to come. And it follows that the United States, in relation to the republics of the Caribbean, can and should use its economic power to assist them in the process of exploiting their natural resources, and expanding their economies. The action that is taken must be wise, and discreet, as well as vigorous. But it is impossible to doubt that, from the broader point of view, assistance to the neighbor states in their efforts to better the conditions of their economic life will redound to the interest of the United States itself. This consideration ought to be borne in mind in everything that follows.

Let us look, first of all, as the necessary background for an understanding of the economics of the good-neighbor policy, at the past relations of the United States with the

Caribbean area. We ought not to attempt to evaluate that policy without some historical perspective; we must take account and rightly assess the forces, some of them still operative, that have played a part in the development of American economic relations with the Caribbean.

This means that we must first analyze the role of American capital in the past evolution of the Caribbean economy. This role was, for a long time, not very important; in the larger part of the nineteenth century America was not, in any substantial degree, a capital-exporting nation. Investments began to be made in Mexico during the rule of Porfirio Díaz, that is, after 1878, and in this same period one of the first great American entrepreneurs began his dramatic career in Central America.

It was Minor C. Keith who, in 1884, secured a very favorable contract for the construction or rather for the completion of a railway across the little republic of Costa Rica, and who secured, as one of the conditions of the grant, vast areas to be used in the cultivation of the banana. Thus began a development which was to have an immense extension in the next two decades. Not only in Costa Rica, but in Guatemala and in Honduras the banana plantations rapidly spread, and by the end of the nineteenth century about twenty companies were engaged in the business. At the same time the tendency towards consolidation made itself felt, and in 1899 was organized the United Fruit Company, which speedily set out upon an ambitious policy of economic aggrandizement in the Caribbean. While it never actually secured a complete monopoly of the banana traffic, it did, of course, often dominate the market, and exercised an immense power over the little states in which its expanding operations were carried on.

In the island republics the analogue to the banana is, of course, sugar. There was a prosperous sugar industry in Cuba even before the revolution of 1895 and the struggle for independence. But the development of the industry was immensely accelerated by the War of Liberation, and American capital began to flow into the islands in increasing quantities in the first decade of the twentieth century. It was favored, of course, by the reciprocity agreement of 1903 which admitted Cuban sugar on relatively favorable terms into the United States; and the immense influence of the American sugar corporations was still further promoted by the collapse that followed the dance of the millions in 1920. That distressful period brought many sugar properties into the hands of American banks; and the representation of American capital in the sugar industry in Cuba not only increased at that time but has tended to increase since.

What is true of Cuba has been true, at one remove, in the Dominican Republic. There the sugar corporations had to wait, for the most part, for the period of the American occupation; but they established themselves at that time, and have expanded their operations since.

Bananas and sugar represent a very substantial part of American investments in the Caribbean. But in the island of Cuba there has been also a very remarkable development of the railroad industry, and of the power industry, both of which have been from the beginning largely, but not exclusively, in American hands. And in addition to these forms of activity there are many others in which American capital plays a subordinate, but by no means wholly unimportant, role. The extent of American investments in the economic life of the Caribbean, excluding portfolio investments, be it understood, was in millions of dollars in 1940 as follows, according to the Office of the Coördinator of Inter-American Affairs in a brochure published in 1944: Costa Rica 24.7; Cuba 559.8; Dominican Republic 442.0; El Salvador 35.3; Guatemala 68; Haiti 12.5; Honduras 66.1; Nicaragua 9; Panama 36.8.

The existence of these aggregations of American capital

in the republics of the Caribbean raises, of course, a fundamental question. How far has the development of these corporate interests been a beneficent influence on the life of the republics? What evils has it brought with it? And what problems does it present from the viewpoint of the present time?

The answer to these questions has to be made with a reasonable sense of historical perspective, but also with a due regard for the social tendencies of the age in which we live. Fifty years ago there would have been found few persons to question the innate desirability of such operations as those which American capital has carried on in the neighbor republics; today there is a not inconsiderable body of opinion, both in this country and in the Caribbean states themselves, which is disposed to be highly critical of these same developments.

On the credit side of the account it must be stated that it is difficult to imagine precisely how *any* substantial development in the great staples could have taken place in the past had it not been for foreign enterprisers. The countries of the Caribbean area, with the exception of Cuba, were simply not in a position to undertake the large-scale investments that are involved in such industries as sugar and bananas. As we have already seen, there is in most of the states with which we are concerned, a distinct shortage of capital funds. To suppose that they could have been found on the scale necessary for the development of forms of enterprise which require very significant basic outlays is to go far beyond the facts.

It is sometimes said that these great investments are no doubt of advantage to American investors, but they are worse than useless from the viewpoint of the inhabitants of the state in which they are made. The profits, so it is argued, are exported; the country itself gains almost nothing. It merely submits to a kind of foreign exploitation in which it has not the remotest interest. It is the innocent victim of a grasping foreign imperialism.

Such a viewpoint derives from a generous sympathy with the less fortunate, and deserves some consideration. It is held by those many persons who today are thoroughly sick and tired of the "trickle-down" theory of economic enterprise, the theory that capitalism is by necessity and by nature thoroughly beneficent, and that all we need to do is to stand still and watch it do its perfect work. But because we accept the thesis that the capitalistic system inevitably involves questions of distributive justice, and that it is desirable that the benefits of that system should not be enjoyed only by the few, it by no means follows that *no* good results can follow from its activities, or that there is no validity whatsoever in the thesis that the benefits of free enterprise are, in some measure, automatically conferred upon the community in general. Without taking that stand-pat position which arouses so much antagonism in so many different quarters, it is possible to demonstrate that the presence of the great American corporations in the republics of Central America or in the islands of the Caribbean *does* confer certain advantages upon the communities within which such corporations carry on their work.

In the first place, it is undeniable that the rate of wages paid, let us say, by the great fruit companies in the Caribbean is higher than that which is paid to most native workers. The gain that comes to the social body from this fact may be possibly offset by the fact that much of the labor employed on the banana coasts has been imported; but even if this fact is admitted it is obvious that whatever is paid out in wages redounds to the general interest of the state. On the one hand, it increases buying power, and tends to the activation of the whole economy. On the other hand, it tends to raise wages in general.

In addition to this fact, the measures which are often

taken by foreign corporations to guard the health of their employees are a positive benefit to the community as a whole. Corporations like the United Fruit build hospitals which, in their standards of operation, are likely to be far superior to those which the local government could itself furnish. They sometimes carry on experimentation in the field of agriculture which is hardly within the resources of the public authorities. They engage in industrial pioneering of a type which would with difficulty be undertaken by the republics themselves. None of these activities are undertaken from pure philanthropy, of course, but the motive which actuates them is not the important thing. The important thing is the social gain which undeniably flows from them.

There is an indirect gain, also, in the building of communications which tend to increase the flow of commerce in general, and to make the people of the Caribbean more accessible to the rest of the world. The establishment of steamship lines, for example, helps to provide markets for all export products, and to facilitate the growth of imports. The building of railroads opens up new areas, and makes possible other forms of economic growth than those directly connected with the foreign industries. The development of transport provides new forms of employment, and thus activates the economic life of the community as a whole.

But beyond and above these considerations, there is something more. It is not by any means true that an industry which exports the greater part of its product is engaged in the impoverishment of the economic body. For one thing, such an industry does not stand still, but under normal conditions often reinvests a part of its capital in the region where it is operating. It is not possible, on the basis of information available, to state statistically the precise extent to which this is true. But of the existence of the phenomenon itself there can be no doubt. Moreover, the foreign dominated industry is engaged in an export trade which provides the means for paying for imports, for necessary imports. Unless one is to undertake to support the extreme view that a purely autarchic development is the best possible form of development, it is impossible to denounce the export of raw materials as an unmitigated evil. It may be true that a healthy state is one in which there exists, within the borders of the country, capital and enterprise adequate for its development. But no one of the Caribbean countries is today in a position where it can possibly attain this desirable objective. Until and unless the situation drastically changes, the role of the foreign corporation within the country cannot be regarded as a purely destructive one.

Finally, at least in theory, the foreign corporation provides a useful source of revenue. There is no reason why, from the abstract point of view, it should not contribute and contribute generously to the advancement of the general welfare through taxation. Indeed, every consideration of social justice suggests that it should do just this. And as the political maturity of the Caribbean states becomes more manifest, and their political strength and stability better founded, this is precisely what is likely to result.

But there is, of course, another side to the matter. The hostility with which great foreign corporations are regarded by not inconsiderable elements of opinion in most of the countries which we are discussing is not due to misguided theory, but to very concrete and definite grievances, and to facts which cannot be denied or minimized. In the first place, the very size of these aggregations of capital constitutes a threat to the independence of the republics themselves. The wealth and power of such a corporate unit as United Fruit is far greater than that of government itself in some parts of Central America. Every people has a healthy and natural distrust of the concentration of economic power in the hands of a few. The existence of such concentration is bound to be felt as a grievance in and of itself. Unfortunately, too, there have certainly been occasions in the past when the administrations of certain Central American republics have been the plaything of American corporate interests, and when the rivalry of such interests has been a powerful factor in keeping these little republics in turmoil. In the period between 1907 and 1911, for example, the numerous outbreaks which occurred in Honduras were undoubtedly due to the machinations of foreign interests, and the same thing was true of the Nicaraguan revolution which broke out in 1909. But the evil does not end there. In the granting of concessions it has not always been easy to protect the interest of the community against the pressure of the American businessman, or to prevent the corruption of officials to the detriment of the welfare of the state. The close tie-up between the great banana interests, on the one hand, and the railroad lines, on the other, has also been the means of exerting an undue pressure on the economic interests which did not align themselves with these powerful forces. And the tremendous wealth of these foreign corporations has made it easy for them to dispose of an influence which may be, and sometimes has been, corrupting and disorganizing. After all, the rule of business is often to get what one can; and the temptations on the one side and the other, on the part of the foreign corporation, and on the part of the venal public official, are difficult to resist. There has been, no doubt, a change for the better in more recent times; but the fact of immense material power is always there, and it is natural that many inhabitants of the Caribbean republics should regard that fact with apprehension and with hostility.

The case against the great foreign corporations can, however, be pushed farther than this. They are not likely to be very sympathetic with projects of social reform, unless, indeed, these projects are of their own initiative; like many

American businessmen elsewhere, they find it difficult to accept the necessity of ambitious schemes for the improvement of the well-being of the masses. It is easy for the corporation executive to sneer at such projects, or to denounce them as merely a means of bringing political pressure to bear upon his own concern; yet nothing is more certain than that in the Caribbean, as elsewhere, there is going to be a process of social change, which, whatever the motives of some of those who advocate it, is deeply rooted in the instincts and the aspirations of our own age. It will never do to flout this passion for self-improvement, or to treat it as merely a matter of political maneuver.

Finally, it is to be said that the influence of American corporate interests has often been, in the very nature of the case, on the side of that monoculture which is one of the limitations of the Caribbean economy. As we have already seen, there is a genuine interest in many of the states in the diversification of their economic life; the foreign corporation buys up and holds idle large amounts of land that might be used for other, and possibly more beneficent purposes; and this fact is bound to mean that from the long range point of view it may find itself at loggerheads with some of the social tendencies which are growing more powerful throughout the area. In particular is this the case with the sugar companies in Cuba; but it may also be true of other parts of the region which we are discussing.

Now what is the conclusion to be drawn from these facts, with regard to the proper attitude to be taken by the Caribbean states toward foreign corporations? Looking at the matter broadly, from the angle of the republics themselves, we must begin by saying that policies which tend to scare away private capital would react in the long run to the detriment of the republics which we are considering. The temptation to exploit a very natural public hostility against "big business" is always there; but to give it free rein would be extremely unwise. It is necessary for the states of the area frankly to face the fact that they cannot live to themselves alone, or at any rate cannot develop by themselves alone; and that the importation of private funds is an essential part of any program of economic advancement. But this does not mean, and cannot mean, that they must permit foreign corporations to dominate the political life of the Caribbean. It does not mean that legislation looking to the amelioration and improvement of the lot of the masses should be held up at the dictates of foreign interests, or that programs of social reform should be indefinitely deferred because they are distasteful to this or that business magnate. In the whole problem of social advance, a nice balance has to be maintained between what is practicable and can be accepted, and policies so radical that they dry up the springs of enterprise and check economic expansion.

But the question of what is proper and desirable is also a question for our own government to consider. And here again there are two extreme points of view that have to be avoided. At one end of the spectrum is the viewpoint that American interests abroad deserve and should receive almost unqualified protection, that the State Department should make itself the aggressive defender of American interests. At the other end is the equally untenable thesis that foreign states should be free to act with regard to foreign interests without interference from their powerful neighbor. The wise course of action lies, of course, between these two extremes. One cannot, under present circumstances and in the present state of judicial administration in the Caribbean, take the attitude that there are no occasions whatsoever on which diplomatic representations by the American government in behalf of American interests are improper. Nor is it by any means certain, in existing circumstances and under the contemporary conditions, that American citizens will not from time to time be harshly treated by the public authorities, possibly unjustly imprisoned, or subjected to other restraints which call for some kind of protest, in one or another of the republics. The same thing, indeed, might happen in many other parts of the world, and might in these, too, call for similar action. A completely indifferent attitude on the part of those in authority at Washington would not be just to our own nationals, nor in the true interests of the states which are our neighbors.

But it is an entirely different thing for the United States to make itself the champion of American business interests against legislation which is well within the competence of any civilized state. And, if the good-neighbor policy is carried out in the future, as it has been in the past, this most emphatically will not be the case. On the contrary, it will be recognized that just as our own country undertook important social reforms in the days of the New Deal, so it will be desirable that the Caribbean republics undertake reforms. And it will not be considered within the bounds of sound policy, from an international point of view, to interfere in a meddlesome way with the progress of the independent republics that are our neighbors. It will be recognized that they have a right to form and to carry out programs of their own; that these programs may adversely affect corporate interests; but that, except in cases of obvious and flagrant injustice, these programs constitute no justification whatsoever for the diplomatic intervention of the United States. This was, indeed, the point of view of the Roosevelt administration; it watched with sympathy the enactment of important reforms in the case of Cuba; it went to the extreme limits of tolerance when the Mexican government expropriated the oil companies; it adopted a similar attitude in somewhat similar circumstances in Bolivia. Such a policy is bound to have its critics; the exact balance that ought to be maintained is a nice one; but at least it can be said that a substantial effort should be made to judge in a tolerant and understanding manner the process of social change outside our borders.

It is, indeed, distinctly arguable that the government of the United States should go even further. It should, perhaps, urge American companies to pursue positive policies of social amelioration, and of consideration for local interests. Mr. Spruille Braden, for example, while our ambassador at Havana, laid down the principle that American corporations should not contribute to the coffers of any political party, and has been applauded for so doing. Our ministers abroad might conceivably go further, and exert a positive influence to see that native labor is well treated, at any rate by the local standard, to do whatever they can to enlist local capital in the various fields of enterprise, to encourage the maximum practicable publicity as to the activities of American business enterprise, to give an impetus where they can to measures calculated to promote the progress of those countries. In particular, the second of the measures mentioned above has large possibilities. The hostility which is sometimes felt towards foreign concerns would be in no small measure alleviated, if not removed, if opportunity were given for Caribbean investors to have a part in the major developments of their own economies on an increasing scale.

To some persons what has just been said will no doubt seem Utopian. If standards such as these are to be set for American enterprisers abroad, will they not prove impossible to maintain in practice? Does not such a view mean that in the future the necessary capital for the development of the Caribbean states will not be forthcoming? Does it not jeopardize their future? Does it not sacrifice to a vague idealism concrete practical interests? Such questions involve a glance into a future that is veiled from all of us. But at least it can be said that there is little in the policy of the governments of the Caribbean states during the last decade to suggest that they have taken advantage of the relative tolerance and restraint of the government of the United States. After all, it is to the advantage of every one of them not to pursue unduly proscriptive policies. They are, in a sense, in competition with one another for the capital which they need for their future development. They are none of them, as we have seen, with the possible exception of Cuba, states in which there exist movements of the extreme Left. Social reform, the impulse to social betterment, they are bound to feel. But drastic change, or a hostility to outside capital so deep as to amount to driving it away, hardly seems likely. Indeed, they are more likely to lag behind than to keep step with, or to go in advance of, the process of social adjustment that is, over a substantial period, likely to take place in the United States.

In the last analysis, of course, no man can tell whether, in the years immediately ahead, there will be an important capital movement into the countries of the Caribbean. There was emphatically such a movement after World War I. The direct investments of the United States in the area increased very substantially between 1913 and 1929. Whether it will do so again depends upon a good many factors, which, in the nature of the case, are variable: upon American business psychology, upon the rate of return to investors at home, upon the demand for funds in other parts of the world, upon conditions, both political and economic, in the Caribbean countries themselves, upon the tempo of world recovery in general. That a continuation of direct private investment in the area is desirable would be generally admitted; but in what form and to what degree it will take place is not a matter upon which confident judgment is possible.

But there is another type of capital movement into the area of the Caribbean besides that of direct private investment for the development of the natural resources of the country. All of these states have, from time to time, had recourse to commercial loans, and many of these loans have been floated in the United States. In the nineteenth century this was hardly the case; but in the twentieth the United States, here as elsewhere, has assumed, not always very intelligently, but by the force of circumstance, the role of a creditor nation. What is the history of this problem, and what the situation as it exists today? In the case of the republic of Cuba, the government has from the beginning of its existence looked to New York when it was in need of funds. Panama, in the nature of the case, followed the same policy. The occupation of Haiti and of the Dominican Republic naturally led to the refunding of the obligation of these two states in this country. In Central America the situation has been somewhat different. Even today the debt of Honduras and of Nicaragua is held in Britain. Guatemala originally looked to London, but later turned to the American money market. Today, however, its debts have been paid off. El Salvador floated an American loan in the period of the twenties. Costa Rica did the same. To put the matter briefly, in three of the nine republics there is today no public indebtedness to the United States. In the case of the other six, the figures are as follows: Cuba, $110,000,000; the Dominican Republic, $14,000,000; Haiti, $5,600,000; Costa Rica, $8,000,000; El Salvador, $4,100,000; Panama, $11,000,000.

It is sometimes assumed that Latin-American states have a uniformly bad credit rating. As a matter of fact, this is by no means the case. The republic of Cuba, for example, has at almost all times maintained interest payments on its debt, with the exception of a single issue, and its record is distinctly good. Haiti and the Dominican Republic have never defaulted on their American borrowings. The three states which found themselves unable to deal with their debt problem during recent times are Costa Rica, Panama, and El Salvador; and the latter two of these have recently made compromise settlements. All of them were, in a sense, victims of the Great Depression and their embarrassment was, in a measure, excusable. For when revenues shrink on a considerable scale, poor governments, such as those of many of the states of the Caribbean, may be faced with the prospect of curtailing the most essential public services, or of postponing interest payments. It is not contended, of course, that their taking the second course is likely to ingratiate the states in question with their creditors, or to improve their standing in the money markets of the world. But the risks of disorder and possibly revolution at home are greater than the damage done to the republics' credit standing by default; at least so the statesmen of the countries concerned are apt to think; and since history seems to show that claims can be compromised, and credit standing restored, their reasoning cannot be regarded as altogether unsound.

The total amount of public loans to the states of the Caribbean, down to the years of the Great Depression, is not, taken as a whole, very great. It amounts to little more than $50,000,000, excluding Cuba, and can hardly be regarded as the basis for any very extraordinary economic development. And in addition to this the question may still be asked whether it will be possible under existing conditions for these republics to borrow freely through private bankers in the future. During the period of the New Deal, and under the good-neighbor policy, it was not the custom of the United States government to constitute itself the defender of the American bondholder who found himself in difficulties because of his holding of Latin-American bonds. It was argued with some cogency that the investor must take the risks and receive the rewards incident to his activity; and while the Roosevelt administration mildly encouraged the creation of a Foreign Bondholders' Protective Council to deal with defaulted issues, it never put itself squarely behind this organization, or gave it much positive support. Taking these facts into account, and recalling also that some of the loans made in the depression period were undertaken by the bankers only at the State Department's suggestion, it does not seem likely that a great flow of private funds into the Caribbean area, in the form of loans, is likely to take place in the near future. Our perspective on this question of private lending is as yet dim; we are too near the war to judge accurately what the tendency will be; but at least it may be said that there is no reason for extravagant optimism.

The drying up of private capital, in fact, produced during the period of the thirties and forties a very substantial amount of public lending, and this process was accelerated by the war. By far the most important agency in the making of these loans was the Export-Import Bank, established by act of Congress in 1934. A list of these loans to the Caribbean states is given in the Appendix. The earliest of them was that to Haiti in 1938, and no one of them was granted after the end of the war.

There are those who believe that the case for public loans, as distinguished from private loans, is an impressive one, both on theoretic and practical grounds. In the past, Latin-American loans were often floated under the most unhappy circumstances. The representatives of the borrowers were often inexperienced, and sometimes venal; they were conscious of being at a disadvantage from the point of view of bargaining power; and they were obliged on occasion to submit to very unfavorable terms. Furthermore, the syndicates that floated these loans often took far too narrow a view of their function; they were too exclusively interested in the opportunities for profit which such loans presented; they were not sufficiently informed as to the possibilities of repayment, and they were unable to judge the advances which they promoted from the standpoint of the improvement of the economy as a whole. Obviously, the same kind of error can be made by the administrators of a public corporation; but since the motive of gain is less important in this case than in the former, there is at least reason to believe that the problem will be approached from a more objective point of view. The actual record of the Export-Import Bank has been so remarkable a one that it tends to reinforce the argument that has just been presented.

There is a second consideration that enters into the account, and gives to public loans a special place in the promotion of the well-being of the weaker states. In effect, what a public loan means is that, to a very substantial extent, the republic to which a loan is extended profits from the borrowing capacity of the United States, and pays a far lower rate of interest than it could secure in the open market. In the earlier days, the rates on loans to the Latin-American states were little short of usurious; they have been less exacting in recent times; but, to give only one example, the little state of El Salvador was obliged to pay no less than 7 per cent for the funds which it sought in this country in 1922. When it is remembered that our own government can and does borrow at less than a third of that rate, the significance of public lending becomes apparent.

In the third place, it may be said for the public as distinguished from the private loan that the former more widely distributes the risk. It is desirable, and no one will question the fact, that loans should be extended only under circumstances where repayment is to be confidently looked forward to. But there is, of course, in such financial transactions no such thing as absolute certainty; and it is better for the loss from a bad commercial transaction to be taken by the whole body of society than it is for it to be borne by a small number of innocent investors.

These arguments are impressive, but they do not tell us, of course, what the future of public lending in the Caribbean area is likely to be. The Export-Import Bank had its capital increased to three and a half billion dollars in 1945. Much of this sum has already either been disbursed, or committed, chiefly the latter, and at the beginning of 1947 the Italian government, which asked for $700,000,000, was given only $100,000,000 from this source. On the other hand, funds flow into the Bank as well as out of it, as borrowers make good on their loans. The statement by the Bank in December 1945 carries a figure of approximately 562 million dollars for funds actually paid out, and no less than 310 million for repayments. It is certainly possible, then, at least in theory, that the Caribbean states should receive some support from this source in the future.

But there is one important reservation to be made in this matter. The Export-Import Bank does not advance money except where it is directly in the interests of American trade. It has, it is true, construed its authority broadly rather than narrowly. But it is in some degree hedged about by statutory restrictions and cannot be expected, therefore, to cover by any means the whole field of foreign landing.

There is, however, another factor in the situation. There has been set up, as a part of the international financial machinery of the post-war period, the Bank for Reconstruction and Development, with a capital of $9,100,000,000. Only a fifth of the capital of this institution is available for direct lending. But the rest of it may be used as a kind of guarantee fund for issues marketed either by the Bank itself or by other public or private agencies. Such an institution may be of very great significance in the future development of Latin America, and of the states of the Caribbean. It has already begun its operations, though no loan has been made to any New World state.

There are, of course, voices raised in the United States against this particular form of international action. While the American government will have a very substantial voice in its affairs, it will, by no means, have exclusive control; and naturally this disturbs a certain type of citizen. But the Bank is there; and even though, in the years ahead, there may be a reaction against what some persons call misguided generosity, and others far-sighted statesmanship in the form of loans, it is difficult to believe that the activities of this new body will be drastically curtailed. If, in addition, it is managed with anything like the competence that has characterized the administration of the Export-Import Bank, there will be very little to fear.

There can be little question that the problem of foreign borrowing is fundamental for the future of the Caribbean. But it is by no means the only way in which the republics of the area can be assisted in the development ahead. The war years, in fact, revealed a great many ways in which the United States might play a useful part in the activation of their economies. There is no reason why some of these expedients, even though they were suggested by the conflict itself, should not be carried over into the years of peace.

Take, for example, the Inter-American Coffee Stabilization Agreement. The situation with regard to coffee production, as has been seen, had been extremely bad in the decade of the thirties. There was chronic overproduction in the industry and wholesale destruction of oversupply in some of the most important coffee-producing nations. The outbreak of the war intensified the problem. The Continental Export market was, of course, curtailed, and, after the fall of France, virtually closed. In these circumstances, the United States took the initiative, and in November of 1940 was signed one of the most far-reaching attempts at hemispheric coöperation ever attempted by the governments of the New World. The guiding principle of the agreement then drawn up was to give to each of the American producers a reasonable part of the American market, on a quota basis, while at the same time providing for relatively stable prices which should not be exorbitant from the viewpoint of the American consumer. The administration of the agreement was placed in the hands of an inter-American Coffee Board, which had its seat at Washington, which was organized under a rather complicated voting system, and which had power to revise quotas, or even to alter prices. The compact thus signed, it must be emphasized, was not, as many previous agreements had been, a cartel, but an agreement in which both consumer and producer interests were taken into account. While, very naturally, conflicting views developed in the actual working out of this arrangement, it has worked on the whole reasonably well and is still in operation in a somewhat modified form.

Also of an emergency nature, but with far-reaching implications, were the various efforts of the American government to develop food-supply programs during the period of the war, carried on through the newly established office of the Coördinator of Inter-American Affairs. Such programs were put into effect in the case of five of the Central American states. Thus, an agreement was made with Costa Rica by which provision was made for the quick production of fruits and vegetables for local consumption and also for packaging and shipment to the American forces in the Canal Zone, and in its execution about 2000 acres of land were brought under cultivation. An agreement of a slightly different type established six demonstrational farms in the republic of El Salvador. In the case of Honduras, there was carried through a major project involving about 6000 acres of land, and in addition to this there was set up a Food Production Service Center, where experimental and demonstrational work in the field of agriculture might be carried on. Similar programs were set in motion in Nicaragua and in Panama.

At the same time that the office of the Coördinator of Inter-American Affairs was initiating these food projects, it was engaged in assisting in the improvement of public health conditions in many of the states of the Caribbean.

In coöperation with local governments, and with substantial contribution from local authority, it attempted to give assistance in the staffing of new hospitals or in the renovation of existing facilities, in the building of health centers and dispensaries, in the stamping out of malaria and other tropical diseases, and in the field of health education. Virtually every one of the neighbor republics, except Cuba and the Dominican Republic, was represented in this program. The sums allocated to it were not large, in view of the need, only three and three-fourths millions, but they at least suggest one method of assistance to the area, the significance of which can hardly be overestimated. There is, as we have already indicated, no more important aspect of the problem of developing the economies of the Caribbean than that of public health.

Of less significance, from a long-range point of view, were the efforts of the United States to promote the growing of strategic materials. At a time when the rubber shortage loomed largest, efforts were made to stimulate the growing of rubber in at least five of the Caribbean states. The most ambitious of these projects was the so-called Shada, undertaken in collaboration with the authorities of the Republic of Haiti. This enterprise, however, did not turn out to be very successful, and had to be abandoned before the end of the war.

It is almost equally difficult to appraise the efforts to develop sources of quinine in Costa Rica and Guatemala, or of rotenone in some of the other Central American states. But whether the possibilities are great or small, it is well to bear in mind that experiments of this kind are useful if they only suggest lines of enterprise and development other than those which have been usual in the past.

It is perhaps important to remark, with regard to all these activities, that the costs are infinitesimal when related to the economic resources of the United States. It is difficult to realize the immense gap that separates us from our neighbors from this point of view. The budget of Costa Rica, to take at random an illustration which will make the point clear, is less than a three-thousandth part of the budget of the United States. The total sum advanced to the countries of the Caribbean in the war years was less than 1/6 of 1 per cent of the American budget for 1947–48, and less than 1/18 of 1 per cent of the budget of the most expensive war year. Sums that seem very small to us, when viewed in the proper perspective, may be highly important to our neighbors, and may constitute a substantial addition to the national income. A million dollars is 2 per cent of the national income of Haiti or Panama, and more than 1 per cent of the national income of every Caribbean state except Cuba, and, by a narrow margin, El Salvador. Such sums, whether loaned or given, have an influence on the economy, both direct and indirect, that it is difficult to measure in comprehending terms, for a people accustomed to think in terms of billions. The indirect advantages to ourselves that may flow from relatively trifling acts of generosity, the gains that flow out to the rest of the world from an advancement in human welfare in any part of it, are additional arguments for the continuation of the policies that have been pursued during the past few years.

There can be little doubt, of course, as one contemplates the various forms of activities that have just been outlined, that the war immensely quickened the spirit of international coöperation with regard to the republics of the Caribbean. But we can go further than this. It has led, as we have mentioned, to the first ambitious effort to deal in a broad and properly coördinated fashion with the almost equally difficult questions affecting the colonial areas of the Caribbean. The constitution of the Anglo-American Caribbean Commission does not of itself guarantee a solution of these questions; but it provides the machinery through which they can be advanced towards solution. The Commission was created in March of 1942; and one of its first acts was the appointment of a Research Council, which should study on a scientific basis the major problems of the Caribbean economy. In addition to the Research Council, there was set up a West Indian Conference, which convened for the first time in March of 1944, and which met again in the spring of 1945. It must not be imagined that the new agencies which have been mentioned have been engaged in nothing more important than discussion— though discussion is itself a useful contribution to action. In the period of the War the Commission did much to stimulate food production in the area: it organized a shipping reserve; it arranged for the bringing of laborers from the islands to the Continent; it elaborated a comprehensive public health program; it made constructive and long-range suggestions with regard to the problems of monocultural agriculture. No doubt, with the war emergency ended, the tempo of its activity may be in some measure retarded; but to say this is only to enunciate the general truth that it is difficult to carry over into peace the kind of coöperation that exists in an emergency situation. It is not only the work of the Anglo-American Commission that stands in danger of being slowed up or even abandoned in the inevitable reaction of a post-war era.

Desirable, indeed, as all these policies of helpfulness are, there exists, of course, a distinct danger that they will be less highly valued in the years just ahead. It is undeniable that there are signs of a reaction. Even while the war was on, Senator Butler of Nebraska, in a speech that was almost unique in the number and variety of its errors and exaggerations, excoriated the policy of handouts to the states of Latin America. He was answered point by point by Senator McKellar of Tennessee, but the viewpoint that had been expressed was doubtless one that pleased some of the Nebraska constituents of the Senator, and that may easily become all too prevalent. There are, it is to be feared, all too many Americans that cannot appreciate the elementary fact that the activation of the economy of other nations may be a very substantial contribution to the well-being of the United States itself.

As a matter of fact, in addition to the projects already mentioned, there are many things that could be done to assist the states of the Caribbean, and indeed the states of Latin America in general, in the difficult period of adjustment that follows the end of every great international conflict. Much could be done, for example, to stabilize conditions by agreements to purchase staple crops; in this early period of peace, much could be done to encourage the purchase of new capital equipment; much could be done to ease the conditions of transport in the face of a world emergency with regard to shipping; much could be done to encourage methods of scientific agriculture. Whoever is interested in the details of these various problems should read the important volume, *Latin America in the Future World*, published for the National Planning Association, and prepared by George Soule, David Efron, and Norman T. Ness. This interesting work treats the problem of the future in a broad and imaginative manner; and without minimizing the obstacles that stand in the way of drastic change in the Latin-American economies makes many constructive suggestions as to policy. What is needed, of course, here as elsewhere, is a broad view of the matters that are involved; and much depends, therefore, upon the degree to which those responsible for our national policy are able to bring such a view to the solution of practical problems. In a world as confused as that of today, and in a period when public attention has been concentrated on the problems of the Old World, and on our relations with the Soviet Union, Latin-American affairs and Caribbean affairs, in particular,

run the risk of being relatively neglected. Yet probably nowhere has there been a more striking advance during the
last few years in the spirit of international coöperation;
and the policy of the United States towards its southern
neighbors has been a remarkable example of the spirit of
generosity and of enlightened self-interest which, if gener-
alized, would go far to make progress possible in the field
of international relations. We can only hope that the gains
that have been made will be kept; and that efforts will be
put forth to enlarge them.

There is one aspect of the good-neighbor policy, in its
economic implications, which we have so far neglected in
this chapter, and that is the matter of freer trade relations.
Such relations, speaking not in a special but in a general
sense, are bound to be of some positive value in assisting and
accelerating the process of world recovery; and in the
period of the Roosevelt administration a notable advance
was made to this end. In the years of the Depression, in particular, governments resorted to all sorts of restrictive practices in the field of international trade in a kind of mood
of desperation; and it is fair to say that the effort to break
the jam was taken up by the Roosevelt administration
shortly after it entered office. The principle upon which it
acted was clear: the President was given authority, by the
Reciprocal Trade Agreement Act of 1933, frequently extended, to lower tariff duties by as much as 50 per cent in
exchange for concessions on the part of other nations, and
it was further stipulated that concessions made as a result
of such agreements should be applicable to all other nations
which did not discriminate against the United States. An
elaborate machinery was devised for the negotiation of such
compacts, with ample opportunities for the interests affected to be heard; and acting under the authority of this
law the administration has concluded agreements with most
of the countries of the Caribbean. Furthermore, by the act

passed in 1945, the President was empowered to make additional concessions, and cut existing duties still further.

The importance of the agreements made under this legislation is not a matter that can be scientifically determined since no one can say with authority just what the course of commerce would have been if they had not been negotiated. It is obvious also that, in the case of some of the Caribbean states producing materials which are not produced at all in the United States such as bananas or coffee, the effect of any international trade pact is not likely to be very far-reaching. But in one specific instance, at any rate, the policy of the Roosevelt administration is of the highest importance. We have already had occasion to stress the immense role which sugar plays in the economy of the republic of Cuba. For thirty years, prior to the advent of the Roosevelt administration, the interests of the Cuban sugar producers were the plaything of American domestic politics. The Cuban revolt of 1895, for example, was in considerable measure produced by the imposition of a tariff on sugar in the Wilson bill of 1894. When the island had been given its independence, arrangements were made by the treaty of 1902 for the admission of Cuban sugar into the United States on a preferential basis. This arrangement lasted for some time; but when the Harding administration came into power in 1921, in the orgy of protectionism that followed, the tariff was raised. The rates of 1921 were bad enough; but the rates of the Hawley-Smoot bill of 1930 were worse. With a reckless disregard for the well-being of a neighbor state, and of American interests in that state, duties were again raised. The misery of the island in 1932 and 1933 we have already commented on.

The trend was reversed by the Roosevelt administration. The rates were reduced unilaterally by Presidential action in June of 1934; in August a trade agreement between Cuba and the United States reduced them still further, the total change being from 2.50 cents to .9 cent a pound. In the same year further constructive action was taken; by the Jones-Costigan Act a fixed quota of Cuban sugar was admitted into the United States. The quota was not so large as the friends and well-wishers of the island republic would have desired; the American domestic and insular producers fared better than did the Cubans. But in the then existing situation the amount that could be imported was more than the Cubans had marketed in this country in the preceding year; and the reduction of the tariff at the same time tended to increase the profits of their operations. Moreover, the quotas were raised in succeeding years, and with the great demand for sugar arising from the war disappeared altogether. Indeed, since 1941, the United States government has contracted for the bulk of the Cuban sugar crop on terms that have not been inconsiderate of the interests of the people of the island. And when the situation changes once again, as change it inevitably will, there is at least a situation in which ridiculously heavy duties—oppressive duties, they may fairly be called—will not enter into the account of our trade with Cuba. It is much to be hoped, in fact, that we shall not again adopt the restrictive policies that operated in the twenties and early thirties. They are policies of national loss, not of national gain, and they have unfortunate political as well as unfortunate economic repercussions among our neighbors. It is certainly not to the interest of the United States to encourage an excessive development towards autarchy in the states to the south; that there should be some readjustment of their economies is intelligible; that Cuba should seek to free herself from dependence on a single crop is desirable; but there is no reason why, in the existing situation, we should add to the difficulties which confront the Cuban government and people by restrictive trade policies.

The pursuance of wise policies towards the Caribbean

states in the future will be more difficult, it may be antici-
pated, on the economic than on the political side. There is
already evident, we repeat, in the year and a half since the
war, a distinct tendency to question the value of assistance
to other states, as merely a kind of misguided benevolence.
We cannot be sure how far this tendency will affect those
responsible for the formation of policy. In the field of tariff
legislation, we are by no means entitled to assume that there
will not be a reaction against the policies of freer trade
that have distinguished the Roosevelt administration. But
whatever the future may bring, we are at least entitled to
take pride in the record of the recent past. It has been,
indeed, a practical demonstration of a general truth, the
truth that the prosperity of any single state is bound up
with the prosperity of all. To say this is not to advocate wild
and uncontrolled extravagance. It is merely to say that the
activation of other economies by judicious measures of public assistance will, in the long run, not only add to the sum
total of international good will, but will advance the practical interests of the United States. Whether we like it or
not, the well-being of the Caribbean states is indissolubly
connected with our own. To take account of this fact may
well be regarded as a simple act of statesmanship. The
example has now been set. What remains is to discover
whether it will be followed.

8. The Psychological Background

In analyzing the relations of the United States with the republics of the Caribbean, in describing the basic political and economic ideas which characterize the good-neighbor policy, we have told only a part of the story. Behind the principles and modes of action we have discussed, there lies something more fundamental than any of them. For at the root of the problem lies the question as to whether in international affairs we can, in the long run, substitute other criteria than those of force and physical power. We may be very sure that such a change, if it comes about at all, will come about slowly. We have no right to assume, from the broader standpoint of America's role as a world power, that we can dispense with the traditional apparatus of armies and navies, or that the immense industrial and war-making potential of the United States is not a factor of great importance in the conduct of foreign affairs. We should recognize, for example, in dealing with the hard-boiled and resolute men who direct the policies of Soviet Russia, that the possession of power has something to do with the playing of the diplomatic game. Whatever may be our desires, we cannot simply put away the instruments of the past and depend upon the broader and more generous motives that play a part in human affairs to do their perfect work. But in dealing with the states of the Caribbean we have an opportunity, and we are using the opportunity, to try what is essentially a great experiment. We have an opportunity to apply the processes of discussion, of consultation, of an appeal to common ideals, to the solution of our diplomatic problems. Power is a great thing, but the moderate use of power, restraint in the exercise of power, is a still greater thing. Nobody can doubt, of course, in these days in which we live, that if we chose to do so we could overawe the states that are our neighbors. We could overawe them not only by the display of our armed might, but by the application of tremendous economic pressure. If the good-neighbor policy is to be continued, however, we are committed to another course of action. We are committed to a genuine effort at international understanding, to an attempt to comprehend the aspirations and the viewpoint of these little states, and to shape our policy so as to reconcile these aspirations and that viewpoint with our own. If we are to do this successfully, we must, above all else, seek to appreciate the psychology of the peoples of these republics, and to accommodate ourselves in some degree, at any rate, to these conceptions. We must not imagine that such an enterprise will be easy, certainly we must not imagine that it will be automatic. It will take effort and time. It is not, as a matter of fact, characteristic of Americans (perhaps it is not characteristic of any people) that they instinctively accept or find themselves in touch with the basic conceptions and characteristics of other nations. The temptation, of course, is to think of our own ways and habits as somehow the best that can be imagined, and to try, in one fashion or another, to force others into our own mold. Yet nothing is really more certain than that nations differ, precisely as individuals differ, that their characters have been formed in a long past, that their views of life, on both the ideal and the practical sides, are the product of their especial experience and environment, and that the right course is to seek an accommodation between differing national psychologies. From many points of view, Latin Americans are not like North Americans, and do not wish to be like us; they have not the slightest intention of being made over in our image; they could not be so made over if they tried, or if we tried.

This is the central fact from which one has to start in discussing the psychology of the two races; and a great deal flows from it. In the field of personal and individual relations, for example, the American is likely to be informal, casual, and sometimes frank to the point of rudeness. The Latin American, on the other hand, attaches great importance to the ritual of politeness, to a certain ceremoniousness, and to a delicacy that avoids wounding directly the pride of those with whom he comes into contact. The American is likely to be extremely energetic, restless, and full of driving energy. The Latin American highly values leisure, and can often see no reason why one should burn oneself out in constant activity. He finds the bustle of the American a bit confusing and disturbing; the American finds his comparative serenity irritating and thwarting. Of course when we say these things we cannot assume to be speaking of all Latin Americans and of all Americans; obviously there are people of all kinds in both societies; but there is enough truth in the generalization we have just been making to warrant its being borne in mind in the field of personal relations.

And personal relations, be it said again, are important. It is a mistake to think of diplomacy as being conducted only at the highest level by frock-coated statesmen who decide great issues of policy. Just as government in a democracy rests on the conceptions of the common man, so international policy rests upon the kind of conceptions of one another that are harbored by the masses of the people in each country. In a sense, every American is a representative of his own nation when traveling abroad; and so he ought to consider himself.

Let us, moreover, be very certain that we do not commit

some of the errors often committed by our fellow-country-men in their judgment of the peoples to the south of us. Most Americans, for example, have a very low opinion of the political capacity of the Caribbean peoples. They are apt to take for granted disorder and venality, and to contrast Caribbean conditions with their own. Some of the elements in the situation are almost completely ignored. The heavy load of poverty which the peoples of these republics are compelled to bear, the difficulties in the way of the spread of popular education, the unhealthy traditions which it takes time to eradicate, are not given their due weight in making up a judgment. That conditions have at least been sufficiently settled, that government has been sufficiently competent to make possible a very substantial economic progress, counts for little or nothing with these hypercritics. That the general tendency is towards greater stability, and towards more imaginative and sympathetic administration, counts for still less. Nor is a backward glance likely to be taken at some of the episodes of our own history. There have been and are venal Latin-American governments, but there was a time, not so very long ago, when the rule of our American cities was a scandal and a reproach. The corruption engendered in this country by national prohibition, and the disregard of law by large and respectable elements in our society during that melancholy experiment, are too often forgotten. Even at this very moment the mayor of one of our largest cities is in jail, and a former sergeant-at-arms of the House of Representatives has been convicted of defalcation. Perhaps we are purer than others, but perhaps also we are not so pure as we like to assume. And when it comes to political comparisons there is hardly any foreigner who is not ready to remind us that in a substantial part of the country a large element in our population is disfranchised and denied the most elementary political privileges on account of the color of its skin.

It is the same way with a judgment on the side of social institutions. Of course, it is true that, by and large, the standard of well-being in the United States is incomparably high, and the desire for social advance is keen. But the vast mass of remediable misery that still exists ought to temper our criticism of others, and the presence of the Negro problem in our midst ought still further to induce a charitable view.

When it comes to the cultural side of life, there is the same tendency on the part of many of our countrymen to depreciate what is done elsewhere, and to exaggerate the significance of what occurs in the United States. We have already seen that there is hardly one of the countries of the Caribbean which has not produced some person of eminence in the cultural field, and in some fields of endeavor the accomplishment of these republics is really quite remarkable, taking into account their resources and the difficulties under which they labor. The members of the educated class, indeed, may often, in their aesthetic appreciation, in the liveliness of their intelligence, in the breadth of their interests, be quite as worthy of admiration as some of the products of our colleges and universities. It will not do to look down one's nose at such people, and it does not make for good international relations to do so. When Americans travel in foreign lands, indeed, they should go to learn, and not to criticize; they should be looking, not for the fortification of their national pride, but for the opportunity to find something they can admire and perhaps imitate. The true principle of international intercourse as of intercourse between individuals is, or should be, mutual teachability. How easy it is for a discussion between persons of different origin to become an attempt to score points on one another; how necessary it is that they should abstain from doing so!

It cannot be said, in the main, that our national press

contributes very effectively to sympathetic understanding of others. No doubt it is better, very much better, that we should have a press that is free than one that is controlled; but the newspapermen who harp on that freedom are as yet by no means as fully aware as they ought to be, speaking of the class as a whole, of their professional responsibility. A short time ago, for example, the foreign minister of a great South American state made to a newspaperman some very critical observations on Soviet Russia at just about the time that a minister from the U.S.S.R. was about to arrive in the state in question; the remarks were, of course, intended to be off the record, but they were promptly published in New York. It is true of most papers that what is sensational in the happenings of another country is what is featured, that drama counts for more than the broad perspective. A balanced budget, a constructive piece of legislation, a peaceably conducted election, a prosperous economy, none of these are very interesting to our average journalist; it is when things go wrong that he eagerly picks up his pen. No doubt, in our domestic affairs, the national common sense is equal to this constant assault upon the national nerves; but in international relations we cannot be so sure. The provincial in every man's character leaps to a critical judgment on the basis of the shortcomings of other peoples that are heralded in the press.

In the same way it is easy for our newspapers to exalt, perhaps unduly, our own national character. It is impossible, in these days in which we live, for any of us, in fact, to be unaware of the immense material and physical resources of the United States. But it is well for us not to harp upon our strength. The powerful are rarely popular because of their power; indeed it is only by their wise use of power that they can make power tolerable. Latin Americans would like to see a world in which law and public morality took the place of power. Because they are weak, their feeling is especially strong on this point. And there can be nothing more offensive to them than vainglorious boasting as to the immense material strength of this country. True, we are a great country, and theirs are small ones; but what of it, they would say? Must we measure nations by size alone? Or should we not accord to the weak and less prosperous the respect that is always due to individual personality?

American politicians constantly offend the pride of the Latin American by contemptuous and irresponsible allusion. Years ago, in the Senate of the United States, I remember a hillbilly statesman from South Carolina who, in the course of a rambling speech, alluded to the representatives of the Caribbean states in Washington as "Halfbreeds." There is, of course, mixed blood in many of the people of this area, but they do not think of it as a matter for contemptuous allusion. Nor do they relish it when other people discuss the matter in this spirit. The speech which Senator Butler of Nebraska made on the goodneighbor policy two years ago was a bad speech, not only because it was full of errors of fact but because running through it all was an ill-disguised contempt for the peoples whom the Senator was discussing. This kind of thing is dangerous, and it is far too common. There are few countries, indeed, in which public men are more irresponsible in their allusions to other nations than the United States. We show some signs of growing up in this regard; but there is still a good deal of maturing to be done, a good deal greater restraint to be exercised.

There is also the danger of what may be most conveniently described as "moral imperialism." The United States, during the recent past, has a very creditable record with regard to the use of force in the affairs of the Western hemisphere. But there are other forms of pressure which are not relished by the peoples to the South.

As we have already suggested, it is doubtful whether the

peoples of the Caribbean will ever really enjoy homilies from Americans on how they should conduct their political affairs, or on the means by which they can improve their economic and political order. They would much prefer to make their own decisions; they would much prefer to come to their own conclusions. They do not want to be redeemed by American statesmen, or American Protestant clergymen, or American college professors, even; and we shall be more effective in influencing them by our example than we ever can be by preachments from the superior altitude of our own virtue. All too frequently this pose of moral overlordship is the position assumed by perfectly good and worthy people in this country; and it does not do much to advance the cause of good international relations.

It is not to be assumed, of course, that the misunderstandings which may arise in our relations with the peoples of the Caribbean are all on one side. They have their misconceptions about us, as we have our misconceptions against them. And those misconceptions, like ours, are a bar to a genuine understanding.

In the first place, it is still far too early for Latin Americans to surrender the idea that the United States is an imperialist power. True, the war with Mexico is now a hundred years in the past; and perhaps it might be conveniently forgotten. But even if it were forgotten, there would still be memories of the interventions which were, after all, brought to an end less than fifteen years ago; and there would still be fears that the events of the years 1912–1934 might reproduce themselves. Furthermore, there are Latin-American politicians, of course, as well as American politicians, who are not above capitalizing a convenient prejudice for domestic reasons, or for personal reasons; and there can be no doubt that striking an attitude, and taking a bold stand against the Colossus of the North, is a pastime that is by no means wholly out of fashion in the republics of the South. To do this, of course, is irresponsible; but this does not mean that it will not be done.

Here at home, of course, we do not feel that these criticisms are justified. To most Americans it would seem reasonably clear that the United States has distinguished itself by its restraint. They would call attention to the fact that hardly any policy in the history of the country has received such widespread support as has the good-neighbor policy. They would stress the fact that at no time was intervention in the affairs of the Caribbean popular, in any broad sense of the term. They would indicate that the United States has been willing, within recent months, to give support to the International Court of Justice set up under the Charter of the United Nations. They would, perhaps, add that, from the point of view of national defense, the agreement with Britain and the construction of bases on the periphery of the Caribbean have removed one of the justifications alleged in the past for the occupation of Caribbean territory. But all these things together would not suffice entirely to exorcise the spirit of distrust that is still felt in some of the states we have been discussing. Unhappily, suspicion is easily aroused, and very difficult to eradicate, and conscious as most Americans are of their own innocence in regard to such matters, it is difficult to convince outsiders.

Another obstacle to understanding is the widespread conviction among other peoples, those of the Caribbean included, that the Americans are a peculiarly materialistic people. It is popular in much of the world to bring forward this cliché, and to inflate it into a major generalization. Certainly no country presents a picture of material prosperity equal to that of the United States. Certainly there is a garish side to American culture, felt by at least some Americans themselves when they come back to the ostentatious wealth of New York City from a visit to "foreign parts." Certainly, Americans, like most peoples today, are much concerned with the functioning of their economic life. Certainly, there are few countries in which business success is so highly regarded and in which it redeems so many sins of selfishness and vulgarity as it does in our own land. But to see these things, and to see nothing more, is to fail to look below the surface. Americans are interested in material things, but they are constantly being moved by ideal motives. Their philanthropies have been as amazing as has the organization of their industry. Their faith in education, and their willingness to support it, are striking illustrations of the value they attach to other things than the purely material. The religious life of America is certainly as active as that of most of the states with which we are concerned in this study. And in the prosecution of the war that ended a year ago, and in the construction of the peace, idealistic motives have played and are playing a role that no informed person can deny. A philosophy of material interest in the past few years might be more easily reconciled with isolationism than with the policy which this country actually followed. No student of American diplomacy, indeed, who has followed the subject with any care, will fail to find many evidences of the force of principle and high purpose in the evolution of American foreign policy. And, indeed, the good-neighbor policy is itself an illustration of the more generous and humane motives that often sway the American mind. It will take time, however, to convince others of the full significance of just such facts; and, needless to say, example will be more important than precept in this regard.

Closely connected with this emphasis on American materialism that figures so often in the thought of other peoples with regard to our own, is the feeling of opposition to "economic imperialism." Here is a term that is nicely calculated to arouse the maximum of prejudice, and to muddy the judgment of many simple people. No doubt there is such a thing as the misuse of economic power, as exploitation, as callous disregard of the economic interests of others. But the difficulty is that to some persons every economic act is charged with just this kind of moral content. A loan, for example, even if badly needed, and granted on generous terms, may seem to the borrower, in his gloomier or more distressed moments, like "imperialism." A foreign corporation's payments to native workers, even if generous by the standard of the country, may look like "exploitation." The Caribbean states need foreign loans, and they need foreign capital. But the very fact that this is so induces a critical and uncharitable judgment with regard to those who furnish the loans, or the capital. And here again is an easy chance for the demagogue to make his appeal to unreason and to prejudice.

All this, indeed, is connected with a fact easily understood, the fact that Latin Americans, those of the Caribbean area no less than others, are excessively sensitive about their independence. At first blush it might seem as if such a thing were impossible; what could be more important than a nation's sense of its own dignity? Dignity, yes; but independence, no. For the plain fact of the matter is that in the world in which we are living today the fact of *inter-dependence* is no less significant than is national autonomy. The states of the Caribbean cannot get along without the United States. They cannot advance without important assistance from this country; they cannot afford to pursue policies that are based on disregard of the purposes and prejudices that exist here. Economic policies that pay no heed to the mores of the Americans would be disastrous; and in the long run political tendencies which arouse irritation in Washington will not be beneficial to those who initiate them. There is little danger that any Latin-American state will be unduly subservient to its great neighbor; there does exist a danger that the value of American friendship may be underrated. It is a temptation to politicians everywhere to exploit the sense of national pride; but it is a temptation that ought to be resisted.

Of the same order of significance is the tendency which may express itself from time to time for Caribbean statesmen to excuse the defects of their political and economic order by reference to American interference. It is, of course, too much to hope that the United States will always use its power wisely, or be helpful in precisely the way that is most desired; but it must be freely admitted that even when the American government acts most judiciously it cannot, of its own motion, effect a fundamental change in the nations to the south. In the last analysis, the improvement of a nation, like the improvement of the individual, depends upon the national character. There is a very human tendency in both cases to look outside for a scapegoat when things go wrong. Such a tendency does not alter the fundamental facts. In particular is this true with regard to one matter to which we have already alluded, but which will bear restatement. One of the most important factors in national progress is the solicitude of the influential and governing classes for the well-being of the less fortunate, and a determination to use the power of government for the amelioration of social conditions. In most of the states we have been considering, as we have seen, there is still a fairly narrow economic base, and a substantial part of the population living in dire poverty, or hardly conscious of the possibilities of economic progress. It will be to the interest of the governing groups in the long run that this situation should be changed. Indeed, unless such interest exists, whatever assistance is rendered will be largely futile and self-defeating. For the attractions of a policy of helpfulness on the part of the United States will soon dim if this helpfulness is seen to mean nothing more than the enrichment of a narrow and restricted oligarchy; it will not be enough that some of the prosperity of this oligarchy trickles down to the less happy; it will be necessary definitely to plan for social improvement on a substantial scale. And the responsibility for such a program rests within, and not without, the republics of the Caribbean. They will never be able to excuse themselves by asserting themselves that they have been hampered in action by selfish American interests, either governmental or private. They are today, in the present climate of opinion, in a position to do more than ever before for the raising of the standard of living of their peoples. What they do will be of immense importance to the future relations of their various countries with the United States.

Does this analysis of the factors that hamper international understanding between peoples whose highest interest it is to comprehend one another induce in the reader a mood of pessimism? It ought not to do so. There is nothing so fundamental in any of what has been said that it offers a bar to good relations. Indeed, it is fairly clear that, in the broad perspective of history, much progress has been made along the pathway of coöperation, and more can be made. But it is not wise, in international affairs, to depend upon some diffuse spirit of benevolence. It is important to analyze, to dissect—and then—to correct.

The psychological divergences between the United States and the people of the Caribbean can in some measure be reduced by the processes of more intimate contact and of education. For example, the State Department has funds to assist Latin Americans who come to the United States with fellowships, or tuition grants, in American universities. Or again, there was signed at Buenos Aires in 1936 a Convention for the Promotion of Inter-American Cultural Relations, under which each country submits to the others a panel of five graduate students or teachers, from which the receiving country selects two to receive fellowships. There are grants, too, for research activities, for travel for writers, artists, educators, and editors, for exchange of professors, for special training. The number of these programs naturally increased remarkably during the period of the war, and may not be quite so impressive in the future. But there is no doubt that much can and will be done from this point of view, and that it will have a very positive practical value. For in the long run such programs are directed towards those elements in society which are likely to be influential in the actual conduct of affairs, and whose good will may be readily translated into a larger practical understanding.

We may expect too, as time goes on, an increasing interest in the states of the Caribbean on the part of the American public. Havana, of course, has been much visited for some time (though certainly not always by those most likely to contribute to international understanding). The Canal Zone receives large numbers of Americans, and brings them in contact with a Latin-American community. There has recently been an intense interest among traveling Americans in Guatemala. A state so picturesque as Haiti is sure to attract more and more visitors, and a visit to Haiti is easily combined with a trip to the Dominican Republic, with its many charms, among them the oldest European-founded city in the New World. Conversely, there is undeniably in the Caribbean increasing curiosity about the United States. The well-to-do classes are likely to appear in this country in larger numbers than in the past.

All this may not be an unmitigated benefit, it must be conceded. The traveling American is often both vulgar and obtuse. His mind is sometimes of the type to which new ideas can hardly be admitted. And, conversely, Latin Americans visiting the United States sometimes see only its less attractive side, the night clubs of New York, or the stockyards, or possibly the crude provincialism of some of our smaller cities. They do not take back, as they might, a sense of the great American virtues, of the spirit of social amelioration, of the passion for self-improvement, of the deep-seated idealism that undeniably affects American foreign policy. And sometimes, no doubt, like our own itinerants, they come to have their prejudices confirmed, and their suspicions strengthened.

But we cannot say that such things are always so. There is much good will in the American temperament, and a very general desire to deal sympathetically with others. Generous judgment is by no means impossible to our travelers. The note of blatant imperialism is almost always absent. And, in the case of visitors to our own country, the fundamental question is not whether we have something admirable to exhibit, but whether, so far as official guidance or individual interest is concerned, we have the wisdom to make certain that it is exhibited. In such matters, tact and understanding are obviously necessary. But such qualities are not so rare that they cannot be mobilized to deal with this particular problem.

At the bottom of this question of psychological relationships, of course, there lies the obvious necessity for an affirmative attitude, rather than a negative one. What can be accomplished by our generation in the improvement of international relations will depend in no small degree upon the attitude which we take towards such problems. Good will and hope are not universal solvents of the ills of mankind. But they are powerful agents in the building of a better international society. They will be as valuable, in the relations of the United States with the peoples of the Caribbean, as they are in every other department of human affairs.

9. The Caribbean and War and Peace

The supreme problems of international politics are the problems of defense in war, and of the consolidation of peace. No study of the Caribbean area would be complete which did not turn its attention to these problems, and attempt to bring them into some kind of contemporary focus. We have already seen how the significance of the area has increased in the last half century, how the building of the Panama Canal gave to it a peculiarly important place in the strategic sense, and how very naturally American policy became more and more concerned with the defense problem in the first and second quarters of the twentieth century. We have also noted, but should note again, the very great historical and practical import of the so-called destroyer-bases deal of the summer of 1940. By that remarkable diplomatic bargain, the frontier of the United States has been thrust forward into the Atlantic. The string of bases which were then conceded to the American government, extending from Newfoundland in the north to Trinidad in the south, affords a degree of protection against attack, either directly from the sea, or indirectly from the air, such as this country has never had before. It is true that, in theory, the possession of these bases is for a period of only ninety-nine years, but as such things go in diplomacy it is fair to assume that they are not likely to be relinquished. In the war that ended in 1945 the Caribbean was not only important in itself but important also because of its relation to the south Atlantic. The circumstances of the time gave a peculiar and vital significance to the "strait" between the African coast and the bulge of Brazil, and the air and sea communication with the bulge of Brazil inevitably involved the inland sea to the north. The line of defense of the United States, it has frequently been indicated, must be considered today as far more extensive than in the past; one of the approaches to this country is by way of Latin America; and the installation of American power in the islands of the Antilles is a measure of security against attack in the future.

So, indeed, it may prove to be. Yet the mind refuses to dogmatize on such matters in such an era as that in which we live. The Secretary of War of the United States, in an important speech only a little while ago, predicted that the next assault on this country would come from over the North Pole. What will be done by directed missile weapons, which may, as the Secretary of War stated, lay waste whole areas, and come hurtling through the stratosphere at immense speed, and from incredible distances, is something on which it is impossible to form a judgment, but on which it is certainly worth while to brood. The historically minded person, committed as he is to the evolutionary point of view of human history, and keenly aware of the fact that mankind seems always to deceive and to contradict the prophets of doom and of utter destruction, is reluctant to believe that the atom bomb and the march of science in general present us with a fundamental problem of almost apocalyptic importance; but the events of our own time undeniably give a new meaning to the problems of diplomacy, and suggest that more than ever before in history it is necessary to do some hard and constructive thinking on the problem of international peace. It is proper, therefore, that we should examine the question as to the role of the

Caribbean states along with the United States, in two great agencies of peace, the Pan American Union on the one hand, and the United Nations on the other.

The Pan American Union is, in essence, no new creation. It came into being, indeed, in the latter part of the nineteenth century, and has perhaps the longest and the most successful history of any important international organization. In its earlier period, it is true, it dealt mostly with nonpolitical problems; but in the course of the last twenty years it has taken on a greater and greater political significance. The seat of the Union has always been at Washington; the Director-General has been until recently an American. Cynical Europeans have been prone to think of this great agency of international coöperation as a kind of instrument of American diplomacy, as one of the weapons in the American armory. Yet such a view would do less than justice to the facts. The states of Latin America, and indeed the states of the Caribbean in particular, have been fully as likely to use the Pan-American movement to check American tendencies that seemed undesirable as to fall into line behind American proposals. At Havana, for example, in 1928, it was the delegate from El Salvador, the distinguished statesman, Señor Guerrero, who led the attack upon the interventionist policy of the United States. At the Conference of Montevideo in 1933, such a state as Haiti was able to use effectively the great international conclave to support the nonintervention point of view. True it is, of course, that during the period of the war, and indeed before the war as the menace of Hitlerian Germany became more definite, there was often exhibited by the states which we have been studying a remarkable solidarity with the United States. Virtually all of them followed this country into the conflict, even before the conference of Rio had affirmed the solidarity of the continents, and made the severance of relations with Nazi Germany a matter of international obligation. True, it is, too, that through the Pan-American machinery many fruitful kinds of coöperation were developed in the years 1941–1945. But to think of these various republics as merely satellites of the United States is completely to misunderstand the nature of this international association. It would be fairer and juster to say that, through the machinery of the Pan-American conferences, our government has committed itself to a procedure which may, and sometimes does, align many of the states of the New World against our own, and which provides a check upon the inconsiderate use of national power. That American public opinion has accepted such a procedure is a matter for gratification, in the fullest sense of the word.

There are certain respects, indeed, in which it is likely to be the case that the policy of the Caribbean states will decidedly not reflect the point of view of some Americans. The use of recognition as a political weapon, for example, is not likely to be regarded with favor by Caribbean statesmen. The suggestion of moral intervention, when it was brought forward by the Uruguayan statesman Rodriguez Larreta in 1945, awakened, as we have seen, no enthusiastic response in Caribbean foreign offices. The publication in February of 1946 of the so-called Argentine Blue Book, in which the Argentine government was held up to public scorn by the State Department, was received in silence by the Caribbean chancelleries. Attempts on the part of the United States to use the Union to develop a policy of moral intervention are not likely to be wholeheartedly welcomed. On the other hand, it is probable that a far more cordial welcome would be given to projects of economic collaboration, that the reciprocal trade program of the United States would meet with a favorable reception in most of the Caribbean states, and that in case of a new and serious physical menace from outside the Americas the experience of the years 1938–1945 would be repeated.

What of the possibility of a threat by one New World state against another? How would the Caribbean republics react to such a danger? How far are they willing to go, to avert such a peril? The question, as is well known, is not an academic one. At the conference which took place in Mexico City in 1945, and which gave birth to the Act of Chapultepec, the nations of the New World agreed to act in concert against any threat of aggression by a New World state. They agreed to accept the principle that "in case acts of aggression occur or there may be reasons to believe that an aggression is being prepared by any other state against the integrity and inviolability of territory, or against the sovereignty or political independence of an American state, the States signatory to this declaration will consult among themselves in order to agree upon measures it may be advisable to take." They further declared that for the period of the war and for an interim period thereafter "such threats and acts of aggression" constitute an interference with the war effort of the United Nations, calling for such procedures, within the scope of their constitutional powers of a general nature and for war, as may be found necessary, including (among others) use of armed force to prevent or repel aggression. And above and beyond all this, they agreed upon the conclusion, at some time in the future, of a treaty by which these various engagements should be carried over into the period of peace.

This fundamental agreement was, so far as it is possible to discover, accepted with very little dissent. As is well known, the drafting of a permanent treaty was delayed, in part because of the United States, which has discouraged the calling of a conference for the purpose. The American government long took the view that it would not sit down at such a conference with the Argentine government until Buenos Aires had taken adequate measures against Nazi influences in that republic. That such a view was shared by many Latin-American governments does not appear. Indeed, the viewpoint itself seems inherently illogical. For the danger of Argentine aggression, if it exists, would be much attenuated by such a treaty as is proposed; and the connection between a pact of this kind and the question of foreign influence in the Argentine does not seem to be particularly evident. At the moment at which we stand, it is not possible to define with accuracy the attitude that the Caribbean republics will be likely to take towards a permanent treaty embodying the principles of the Act of Chapultepec; but there is no good reason to believe that they would be hostile to such a pact, any more than they were hostile to the idea at Mexico City two years ago.*

Since the Act of Chapultepec was signed, there has come into being, however, a larger and more general instrument for the preservation of peace, and a larger and wider international organization than the Pan American Union. The Charter of the United Nations was drafted at San Francisco in the spring of 1945. The United Nations Organization itself came into being before the year was over. What will be the role of the Caribbean nations in this great experiment, and especially in their relations with the United States?

As in the case of the Union, there is no reason whatsoever to believe that the Caribbean states will be nothing but echoes of the American government. They certainly did not so behave at San Francisco, itself. They did not so behave at the meeting of the United Nations Assembly in New York in the fall of 1946. They are not likely so to behave in the future. As small states, they are likely to attach a good deal of importance to asserting themselves against the larger ones. Cuba, for example, at the United Nations Assembly, took a very strong position against the so-called veto, against that provision of the Charter by which the five great states can virtually prevent action on

* How they stand will soon be determined at the forthcoming conference at Rio de Janeiro.

all questions but a question of procedure in the Security Council. Our own government was much more restrained and cautious, and there is no reason whatsoever to think that its attitude was insincere. Indeed, it is not the Caribbean states alone that enjoy the opportunity of a show of independent action which the Assembly affords. We may expect, and should indeed approve, a somewhat confident tone on the part of the less powerful, and a certain tendency to call the great to account. The tendency is an almost unqualifiedly hopeful one.

Of course there does exist on many questions a genuine identity of outlook between the United States and its neighbors. And on some occasions, and in some fashion, it may be that there will be a tendency over the long term for our own government and theirs to act together. If in international gatherings, either in the Security Council, or the Assembly, there is a sharp divergence between the views of Soviet Russia and the views of the United States, it *does* seem highly probable that the republics of the Caribbean will in the main align themselves with this country. And this fact will no doubt be highly irritating to the statesmen of the U.S.S.R. In fact, at the conference of San Francisco Mr. Molotov made no particular attempt to disguise his feelings on this point. The tone of voice in which he spoke of the "delegate from Honduras" suggested that there was no particular reason to respect the judgment of that individual. In the Assembly there are a big number of votes from the Latin-American countries. And if these are cast pretty steadily against the views of the Soviet Union, we must expect to hear accusations that some of these states, at least, are not free agents.

There is, of course, no way to convince the suspicious that their suspicions are unjustified. The Russians are themselves too adept in the playing of bloc politics not to attribute the same technique to others. If they wish to believe the worst, they are privileged to do so. The most that the

United States can do is to avoid giving any genuine foundation for such a charge. And there are signs that the State
Department is aware of the danger, and that it intends to act
as circumspectly as possible to avoid giving a handle to this
accusation of collusion. It will be much better for the new
Organization if the Latin-American states, the Caribbean
states among them, not only appear to act freely, but do act
freely. We do not want them as satellites; we want them
as friends—and sometimes as candid friends.

In one respect, moreover, they may well have a positive
role to play of substantial importance as time goes on. Strong
emphasis is likely to be placed by all of them on peaceable
procedures for the settlement of international disputes, and
especially on the codification of international law and on the
encouragement of international arbitration. Both of these
objectives are highly desirable, if viewed in their proper
relationship to the problems of international relations as a
whole. There is every reason, if the thing can be done, to
widen the area in which fixed legal principles can be applied
to the solution of international difficulties. There is every
reason, so far as is feasible, to encourage and extend the
use of arbitral procedure in international affairs. It is obvious, of course, that there are limits beyond which, at the
present time, this program cannot go. But the United Nations
Charter provided specifically for an International Court of
Justice and the Court has been set up. The Senate of the
United States has accepted its jurisdiction in disputes of a
juridical character (with a vague reservation). It is within
the bounds of American statesmanship to use this agency
more and more, and to contribute through it to the strength-
ening of the machinery of peace. In any such course it is
probable that the American government can count upon the
cordial support of the states of the Caribbean.

It is also likely that the economic institutions of peace
will receive support from our neighbors. They have an
interest in such an agency as the International Bank; they

have an interest in broadening the area of economic co-operation. And, as has already been said, it may well be the case that in the period immediately ahead of us some such public international agency for the granting of loans may be an essential element in the process of reconstruction.

Nor can we by any means overlook the natural idealism of the Latin-American temperament with regard to peace in general. There have been wars, international wars, in Latin America as in other parts of the world. But in the Caribbean area there has not been such a war for nearly forty years. And there has been only one major conflict, and that between only two states, in the twentieth century, in any part of the Latin-American area. In the support of the cause of world peace, the statesmen of the neighbor republics may well play an honorable part.

Obviously, their role cannot be a decisive one. The transcendent issue of the world we live in today, one which calls for the greatest patience and wisdom and understanding, is the adjustment of the divergent interests and ideals of two great world powers, the U.S.S.R. and the United States. On the statesmen of the two countries there rests the heaviest burden of responsibility, and on their decisions the fate of humanity in the future may turn. But one of the agencies which may help to bring them together is the United Nations; and the spirit that can bring them together is the spirit of the Americas. In the New World our country has evolved a foreign policy which meets both the practical test and the test of ideals. In seeking on a wider stage that reconciliation of views which is the price of peace, and of international understanding, the United States may well be assisted by the opinions of its neighbors. Theirs is not the voice of power; but it may be the voice of reason. And to give to reason and fair play a wider scope in the field of international politics is the task of enlightened statesmanship today.

Appendix I. Some Vital Facts About the Caribbean

SOME ESSENTIAL STATISTICS ON THE CARIBBEAN COUNTRIES*

Country	Population (estimated)	Area (sq. miles)	Density (per sq. mi.)	Budget (converted into dollars)	Dollar Expenditures per Capita
Costa Rica	746,535	19,233	38.8	$ 11,563,500 (1945)	15.49
Cuba	5,051,850	44,218	114.2	163,880,000 (1946)	32.44
Dominican Republic	1,940,546	19,332	100.4	26,333,644 (1946)	13.57
El Salvador	1,934,925	13,176	146.9	14,927,200 (1946)	7.72
Guatemala	3,546,624	48,290	73.4	34,095,000	9.61
				(July 1947–July 1948)	
Haiti	2,719,474	10,714	253.8	7,276,120	2.68
				(Oct. 1945–Sept. 1946, and this budget carried over into Dec. 1946, since no new budget law had been passed)	
Honduras	1,201,310	59,161	20.3	5,580,927	4.65
				(July 1, 1944–June 30, 1945)	
Nicaragua	1,070,475	57,915	18.5	10,823,000	10.11
Panama	687,952	28,575	24.1	30,266,518	44.00
				(July 1, 1945–June 30, 1946)	

* All statistics are the latest available ones. The Division of Economic Information of the Pan American Union furnished all materials except those dealing with the Disbursements of the Export-Import Bank. These were taken from the *Report to Banking and Currency Committee of the House of Representatives*, 1945.

AMERICAN INVESTMENTS IN THE CARIBBEAN

Country	U.S. Direct Investments (Dec. 31, 1940)	U.S. Dollar Bonds Outstanding (as of 1945)	Export-Import Bank Disbursements June 15, 1945
Costa Rica	$ 24,726,000	$ 8,093,976	$ 7,174,607
Cuba	559,797,000	95,853,900	45,678,473
Dominican Republic	41,895,000	16,292,000	3,283,932
El Salvador	11,204,000	8,846,425	900,000
Guatemala	68,224,000	878,000	
Haiti	12,479,000	6,684,315	10,320,000
Honduras	38,267,000 *		895,000
Nicaragua	8,858,000		4,400,000
Panama	36,815,000	15,640,519	2,487,704
Totals	$802,265,000	$152,289,135	$75,139,716

* This includes British Honduras.

U.S. TRADE IN THE CARIBBEAN AREA

Country	Exports to U.S.	Imports from U.S.
Costa Rica	$ 7,801,316 (1944) 9,805,808 (1945)	$ 14,437,056 (1944) 18,739,929 (1945)
Cuba	386,092,591 (1944) 323,330,537 (1945) 320,684,262 (1946)	160,904,016 (1944) 177,797,106 (1945) 227,432,881 (1946)
Dominican Republic	13,170,707 (1944) 11,749,292 (1945)	13,170,707 (1944) 14,582,521 (1945)
El Salvador	14,927,200 (1944)	8,389,874 (1944)
Guatemala	20,761,055 (1944) 27,596,273 (1945)	12,744,129 (1944) 15,744,475 (1945)
Haiti	10,485,103.80 (Oct. 1943–Sept. 1944) 13,302,541.60 (Oct. 1944–Sept. 1945) 14,138,639.20 (Oct. 1945–Sept. 1946)	11,124,710.80 (Oct. 1943–Sept. 1944) 10,737,678.40 (Oct. 1944–Sept. 1945) 13,687,539.20 (Oct. 1945–Sept. 1946)
Honduras	7,922,184.95 (July 1, 1943–June 30, 1944) 9,897,337.02 (July 1, 1944–June 30, 1945)	8,720,930.55 (July 1, 1943–June 30, 1944) 10,547,016.73 (July 1, 1944–June 30, 1945)
Nicaragua	14,061,417 (1944) 12,571,818 (1945)	7,601,073 (1944) 8,926,364 (1945)
Panama	2,495,996 (1944) 3,970,050 (1945)	25,190,819 (1944) 28,520,926 (1945)

Appendix II.   Suggested Reading

The books suggested below are, of course, only a small part of the literature in the field. They constitute, however, a list that will effectively supplement this volume, and provide a sufficient body of material for a more intensive study of the subject. In particular, they include the most important and most recent works.

BACKGROUND

Though there is a voluminous literature on the Caribbean, the first step toward an understanding of the area may well lie through certain general works that deal with all of Latin America. On the side of geography, for example, Preston James's *Latin America* (New York, 1942) is a study of wide and accurate scholarship. In the field of diplomatic history, Samuel F. Bemis' *The Latin American Policy of the United States* (New York, 1943) is equally valuable. For economic relations, Paul R. Olson's and C. Addison Hickman's *Pan American Economics* (New York, 1943) is by far the ablest synthesis of materials, and contains important statistical information as well as much else that is valuable. *Latin America in the Future World* (New York, 1945) by George Soule, David Efron, and Norman T. Ness is an analysis of the possibilities of the whole continent from the point of view of a group of confirmed liberals. It is at times a little exalted in tone, but it is the most socially minded and advanced of any of the general works, and it is packed with data on the social and cultural situation of the various republics of Latin America. Seymour E. Harris, ed., *Economic Problems of Latin America* (New York and London, 1944), contains much valuable material. An interesting study on a specific phase of our relations is Willy Feuerlein and Elizabeth Hannan's *Dollars in Latin America* (New York Council on Foreign Relations, 1941). For an authoritative discussion of the good-neighbor policy, readers should certainly study the chapter on it in *The Time for Decision* (New York, 1944) by Sumner Welles, who had much to do with fixing the standard and method for American action.

If we move from the Latin-American continent to the Caribbean itself, there are three scholars who have written general studies of this area, and whose works deserve to be noticed. J. Fred Rippy has written *The Caribbean Danger Zone* (New York, 1940), which is interesting on all accounts, and especially worth while for those who would like to confirm their prejudice against international bankers. Dana G. Munro is the author of a small volume, *The United States and the Caribbean Area* (Boston, 1934), which is almost entirely limited to the political side of our relations with the Caribbean republics, but which is excellent of its kind. Chester Lloyd Jones' *Caribbean Backgrounds and Prospects* (New York, 1931) is the most useful of several works on the area by this author, and supplements Munro and Rippy.

INDIVIDUAL STATES

When it comes to the individual states, Charles E. Chapman has written *A History of the Cuban Republic* (New York, 1927), which carries the story down to 1925. The author is none too sympathetic towards his subject, and is unduly shocked by the weaknesses which the Cubans reveal, and by their failure to act like middle-class Methodist Americans. But his work is nonetheless the best history of the republic that we have. Russell Fitzgibbon's *Cuba and the United States, 1900–1935* (Menasha, Wis., 1935) traces Cuban-American relations from 1900 to 1935, and is in every way excellent. Whoever would understand the sugar question in detail should certainly read this book. Leland H. Jenks's *Our Cuban Colony* (New York, 1928) is highly critical and goes down only to the twenties, but is suggestive and raises some of the fundamental questions. Extremely valuable, and indeed almost without parallel, is the *Problems of the New Cuba* (New York, 1935), the report of a Commission on Cuban Affairs, prepared at the request of President Mendieta, and under the direction of Raymond Leslie Buell, who was at the time President of the Foreign Policy Association and chairman of the Commission. Dr. Buell assembled a remarkable group of experts, and the report is far and away the most comprehensive analysis of Cuban affairs that can be found.

There are a number of very interesting works on Haiti. James G. Leyburn's *The Haitian People* (New Haven, 1941) is a sociological study, oftentimes penetrating in analysis, and somewhat gloomy (perhaps rightly) in tone. A highly sympathetic discussion of the folkways of the Haitian peasant is Melville Herskovits' *Life in a Haitian Valley* (New York, 1937). On the more popular side, but written with great charm, is Blair Niles's *Black Haiti* (New York, 1936). The key work on relations with the United States, coming down to the end of the thirties, is Ludwell Lee Montague's *Haiti and the United States, 1714–1938* (Durham, N. C., 1940). If one is interested in a scholarly and often provocative analysis of the period down to 1891, one should look at Rayford W. Logan's *The Diplomatic Relations of the United States with Haiti, 1776–1891* (Chapel Hill, 1941). For the occupation, there is a most useful and careful study by Arthur C. Millspaugh, *Haiti Under American Control, 1915–1930* (Boston, 1931). The author was for a time an administrator in Haiti. Another judgment on the occupation, and one all the more impressive since it was written from a critical viewpoint but finds much that is good, is *Occupied Haiti* (New York, 1927) by Emily G. Balch and Others.

On the Dominican Republic there is a study of very great importance for the historian in Sumner Welles's *Naboth's Vineyard* (New York, 1928), which deals in detail and most sympathetically with Dominican history down to 1924. Melvin M. Knight, *The Americans in Santo Domingo* (New York, 1928) is written with a considerable animus against the ways of American imperialism, but it is a valuable if not always a just critique, and it contains a historical review of American-Dominican relations. The author is among those who judge with excessive harshness the migration of American capital into the undeveloped countries of the Caribbean.

On Central America there is a truly classical study by Dana G. Munro, *The Five Republics of Central America* (New York, 1918). This book, though written almost thirty years ago, is a model of its kind, and contains much interesting information that is relevant today. It stands without a rival in its field. There should also be mentioned Charles D. Kepner and J. H. Soothill's *The Banana Empire* (New York, 1935), which is too much concerned with the sins of the United Fruit Company to present a well-balanced picture, but which deals with politics as well as economics and throws much light on an industry which is vital to the health of Central America. If something lighter is desired, Wallace Thompson's *Rainbow Countries of Central America* (New York, 1926) will supply the need. There have recently appeared two books on Central America by Charles Morrow Wilson, one entitled *Challenge and Opportunity: Cen-*

tral America (New York, 1941), and the other *Middle
America* (New York, 1944). Mr. Wilson, a propagandist
for the development of these regions, writes with an enthusiasm that sometimes outruns judgment. But his book contains
much information that is not to be found elsewhere.

Material is somewhat scarce on the individual countries.
Guatemala, the most picturesque of them all, is the best
described. Chester Lloyd Jones's book on this country,
Guatemala, Past and Present (Minn., 1940), is well worth
reading, and many-sided in its view. Honduras, the most
backward of the states, has been neglected. Nicaragua's
relations with the United States are painstakingly treated
in I. J. Cox, *Nicaragua and the United States, 1909–1927*
(Boston, 1927). And interesting, as a revelation of method
and personality, is Henry L. Stimson's *American Policy in
Nicaragua* (New York, 1927). But, in view of the promise
of this little country, it is a pity that there is no detailed
study of it. El Salvador is discussed in P. F. Martin's *Salvador
of the Twentieth Century* (New York, 1911), but this book,
though useful, is by now too old to be just what one would
want. Costa Rica is better dealt with. Chester Lloyd Jones's
Costa Rica and Civilization in the Caribbean (Madison,
1935) is an excellent study, and one that is highly sympathetic in tone. John and Mavis Biesanz's *Costa Rican Life*
(New York, 1944) is a kind of Costa Rican *Middletown*,
but without the genius that distinguishes the Lynds. It is,
however, distinctly worth while.

Panama needs an analyst of the first order. There is an
old book, *Panama of Today* (New York, 1927) by A. H.
Verrill. For those who are interested in the circumstances
under which the United States acquired title to the Canal
Zone, the most recent and the most balanced and authoritative study is that of Dwight C. Miner, *The Fight for the
Panama Route* (New York, 1940). Those who prefer ro-
mantic narrative to the facts, and wish to get in touch with

a most interesting and vital personality who played an important part in the events of 1903, should read Philippe Bunau-Varilla's *Panama: The Creation, Destruction and Resurrection* (London, 1913).

KEEPING UP TO DATE

It is no easy matter to keep up to date on the Caribbean. The best source, no doubt, is the yearbook, *Inter-American Affairs* (New York, 1942), edited by Arthur P. Whitaker. This deals with every aspect of Latin-American life, and its articles are written by a carefully selected group of specialists. The *Bulletins* of the Pan-American Union (Washington, 1907–   ) are invaluable and cover almost every aspect of Latin-American affairs. Of scarcely less value is the bimonthly *Commercial Pan America*. Many of the readers of this book will be already familiar with the publications of the Foreign Policy Association, located in New York City. Those who are not will find its weekly bulletins, its reports, and its booklets an invaluable assistance in the current study of international affairs.

There are, of course, general sources that ought not to be neglected. Obviously, in the newspaper press, no other paper carries the amount of news on international relations that is to be found in the columns of *The New York Times*. The magazine, *Foreign Affairs* (New York Council on Foreign Relations, 1922 to date), is an invaluable aid to every student of American foreign policy. A quarterly of wide reputation, it stands in a place by itself for penetrating and impartial treatment of foreign policies, and questions related to them. The *International Year Book* (New York, 1908 to date) has articles on the Latin-American republics which are far fuller than those of any other annual publication of a general character.

INDEX

INDEX

Export-Import Bank, 193, 194–196

Exports, major, from Caribbean area, 42

Farmer's Union, Costa Rica, 98

Farrell, General, 169

Fascism, 97; in Caribbean countries, 95. *See also* Totalitarianism

Fernández, Mauro, 106

Feudalism, 34

Fiallo, Fabio, 112, 142

Finlay, Carlos, 109

Fonseca, Bay of, Nicaragua, 131

Food Production Service Center, 197

Food-supply projects, 197

Foreign Bondholders' Protective Council, 192

Franco, Francisco, 94

French Revolution, 119

Fruit, Caribbean staple, 41–42

Fuehrerprinzip, 88

Full Employment in Great Britain (Beveridge), 177

Galicia, 20

Gatun, Lake, 5

Geography, of Caribbean region, 5–7

Germans, in Guatemala, 22; docility of, 92

Germany, 172, 174; in Caribbean, 125

Gold, Nicaragua, 38

González, Colonel, 78

Good-neighbor policy, intervention, 133–145, 147–150; defined, 146; Roosevelt emphasizes, 150; principles of, 159–164; nonrecognition, 167–171; consultation, 171; nonpartisanship, 172; economic background, 178–180; freer trade relations, 202–205

Granada, Nicaragua, 74

Grant, Ulysses S., 121

Grau San Martín, Dr. Ramón, 78, 99, 151–153

Great Britain. *See* Britain

Great Depression, 62, 76, 99, 174, 175, 178, 192

Greytown, Nicaragua, 135

Guadeloupe, 3; Negroes in, 9

Guantánamo, Cuba, 123

Guardia, Tomás, 67

Guatemala, 4, 84, 114, 168, 191, 219; Indian question, 12–16; mestizo element, 18; white stock, 20; German immigrants, 22; population density and birth rate, 26–27, 32; chromium and antimony, 38; landownership, 38–39, 40–41; corn crop, 41; economic diversification, 50; communication facilities, 53–54; automobiles, 55; national income, 57; war-time inflation as cause of unrest, 61; political history, 71–73, 85; labor movement, 103; income and expenditure, 104–105; literacy, 107; newspaper circulation, 108; doctors, 109, 110; hospital facilities, 110; religion, 116; banana plantations, 179; American investments, 180; quinine, 198

Guatemala City, 6, 113

Guaxachip Bats, Indian rites, 13

Guerrero, Señor, 223

Haiti, 3, 4, 147, 219, 223; climate, 6; Negro state, 8–9; white strain, 21; population density and economic outlook, 27–31, 32; lack of raw materials of industry, 36; bauxite deposits, 31, 37; landownership, 38; economic diversification, 49; highway system, 52, 140; automobiles, 55; national income, 57;

inflation in World War II, 60;
republicanism in, 63–64; political history, 81–82, 85, 86; Communist movement, 99; indifference to peasantry, 102; income
and expenditure, 104–105; education, 105–106; literacy, 107;
newspaper circulation, 108;
doctors, 109, 110; hospital facilities, 110; culture, 112, 113; religion, 114–116; American intervention, 133, 136–137, 138–
141, 142–143, 144, 150; education, 140; public health, 140–
141; American investments,
180; American loans, 191, 193;
Shada project, 198

Haitian Bank, 136, 137

Haitian People, The (Leyburn),
quoted, 28–29

Harding, Warren G., 128, 203;
opposes interventions, 147–148

Harris, Seymour, quoted on unemployment in Latin America,
61–62

Havana, 113, 149, 219

Havana Conference, 153, 157–
158, 223

Havana, University of, 76, 107

Hawley-Smoot bill (1930), 130,
203

Hayes, Rutherford B., 122

Hearst, William Randolph, 123

Henriques Ureña, Pedro, 112

Heureaux, Ulises, 79

Highways, Cuba, 51; Dominican
Republic, 52, 140; Haiti, 52,
140; Honduras, 52–53; Panama,
53; Nicaragua, 53; El Salvador,
53; Guatemala, 53; Costa Rica,
54. *See also* Pan-American
Highway

Hitler, Adolf, 90, 91, 94, 165,
172, 174

Honduras, 4, 130, 147, 168, 191;
Negro population, 11–12; mes-

tizo element, 18; white stock,
20; population density and birth
rate, 26–27; silver mining, 37–
38; landownership, 40, 41; economic diversification, 50, 51;
highways, 52–53; automobiles,
55; national income, 57; inflation in World War II, 60;
political history, 75; dictatorship, 91; income and expenditure, 104–105; literacy, 107;
newspaper circulation, 108; doctors, 109; hospital facilities, 110;
internationalized, 126; banana
plantations, 179; American investments, 180; machinations of
foreign interests, 185; food-supply project, 197

Hookworm, 7, 109

Hoover, Herbert C., 129, 130,
150, 151, 178

Hospital facilities, 110

House of Burgesses, Virginia, 82

Huerta, General Victoriano, 169–
170

Hughes, Charles Evans, 148, 149

Huipiles, 113

Hull, Cordell, 154

Huntington, Ellsworth, cited on
tropical indolence, 7

"If I Were Dictator" (Jones), 84

Immigration, lack of, in Caribbean region, 22

Imperialism, American, 122; financial, 133–134; moral, 212–214;
economic, 215–218

Imports, United States, from Caribbean, 43–44

Income, national, of Caribbean
countries, 56–57, 103–104

India, population increase and
standard of living, 24

Indians, in Caribbean region, 12–
18

Industry, agriculture and, in